Pushing Forward

A Memoir of Motivation

Randy Snow

KENDALL/HUNT PUBLISHING COMPANY
4050 Westmark Drive   Dubuque, Iowa 52002

Contents

Foreword

These pages contain a talisman of accounts, testimonials, and experiences of the wheelchair athlete. The traumatic articulation from being able-bodied to wheelchair-bound, together with the happiness, success, sadness, and failure associated with this "last minority" are portrayed in this heretofore-unparalleled treatise.

All people, be they athletes or not, be they able-bodied or disabled, will benefit from the assimilation of this monograph. Since Randy Snow's farming accident in 1975 left him a paraplegic, he has systematically become one of the world's greatest wheelchair athletes, and unquestionably the greatest wheelchair tennis player of our time.

Randy Snow's life experiences have defined leadership, organization, spirit, and discipline. When he was a success he added to it. When he was a failure, he came back. Now these renditions can encourage those who read them to apply the principles gleaned for success in their own lives, in their jobs, within their families, or in a thousand forms of competition.

If asked, the first thing that comes to mind about Randy Snow, it's easy—"Courage"! If asked the major difference between the able-bodied and the disabled, it's easy—"There is no difference"!

Legend has it that when Randy Snow won his 10th U. S. Open Wheelchair Singles title, God appeared to him and said, "Randy, you've done a good job. You can have your legs back." Randy quickly replied, "Lord, can I play just one more tournament?"

Dr. Ballard Moore

Acknowledgments

Many wonderful people have crossed my life. Listed below are significant individuals or groups who have touched me in a very special way. To those I've forgotten, please accept my apology, for my appreciation still exists.

I am indebted to my family who I am very blessed to have... I love you.

I must thank the National Wheelchair Sports Fund and Bruce and Verena Karr, not only for providing a mechanism to self-esteem for literally thousands of people with physical challenges, but also for the support they have provided me personally and for this book.

My apprenticeship with my friend Dr. Bal Moore has been intensely meaningful, of which words cannot describe. Coach, I knooowww!

I am a better person because of my relationship with Marilyn Hamilton and the Quickie Designs people, David Kiley, Skip Wilkins, Jim Black...my appreciation is firm.

Recognition goes to my good friends Shorty Powers and Mark Hamman for tolerating me at times like a mouth does a hot bite of pizza. They are paragons of unconditional friendship.

To Craig Rehabilitation Hospital, Beverly Parrot, Joe Gomez, Dr. Mentor and the staff: I will always be obliged to them for teaching me their version of *pushing forward*.

I would like to recognize some of my coaches *along the way*...David Bohrnstedt, Frank Burns, John Chambers, Judy Einbinder, Susan Finklestein, Jim Hayes, Brad Hedrick, Dan James, Bruce Karr, the Kniffens, Wayne Leavitt, Ron Labar, Joe Moss, Jim Moortgat, Fernando Sarife, Lew Shaver, Lea Sauls and of course Bill Hammett...they are all a part of me.

Also I would like to thank the counselors at Hazelden and CTTC, the boys at Oxford House-Trotwood, Bruce Scott, Sammy Rizzotto, Sarah Cowen, Patsy Snyder, Doug Yule, Mike Haynes and the Austin Wreckers...for believing in me during difficult times.

To Ed Madden at Sterling International Speaker's Bureau, thanks for getting me going.

A mention of appreciation goes to my grammar committee... Alison Norton, Tina Dale, Bal Moore, Virginia Rose, Walt Dudley, Mark Null and Tom Snow, for their help in previewing this work. Let it be known that anything found incorrect or offensive, they suggested I change, but being steadfast I chose to keep.

Finally, acknowledging the many lessons that lie in the belly of adversity, this book is for the *underdog*.

✳ *Pushing Forward is dedicated to my sister's kids.*

Introduction

Over the 1990–91 tennis season, I had won 68 matches in a row, 15 straight tournaments and was on my way to winning 2 gold medals in Barcelona. I was the king of wheelchair tennis.

But as life places us on extraordinary ascending pathways, where things are going so smoothly we *think* we have it all figured out, it can also take us to the down side of advantage, like the prison of paralysis, where we wonder *what our next move is?*

I was training for Sydney, my fourth Paralympic games and was hitting lots of balls…racket back, preparation, "see the seams", follow through…focusing on the most important thing in tennis and in life…*nothing*. The environment was the usual with the sounds of a ladies tennis league, a blue bird sky and windless day, the resonance of the pressure building in the machine as each ball fell into the shoot, then the "whoosh" as it passed through the rollers on its way to me. But in the background for over an hour, I could faintly hear the echo of a ball being hit.

I acquiesced with a glance and saw this kid hitting a ball against a backboard, over and over. He was a little boy, about seven, with a beige hat, striped shirt and blue shorts, and a racket and one faded tennis ball. I couldn't see his face as his hat was pulled down over his brow. I stopped training and my mind began to drift. How many times had I done the same thing, trained by myself in innocent youth and sport for hours on end? I drifted further… wondering…

What if that boy were to break his back someday like me, and have to abruptly stop everything he was doing and had planned to do? What if his early dreams of athletic and personal success were permanently derailed, forcing him to learn how to dress again, at sixteen years old? What if he had to deal with excruciating pain, constant stereotypes, inaccessibility, and social ignorance? God, I hope not.

Yet what if he was able to participate in Olympic competition and know what it was like to represent his country? What if he was able to influence the presidents of companies and countries? What if he was able to help change the attitudes of millions of people around the world through sport, encouraging people to focus on what they had rather than dwell on what they didn't? God, I hope so.

I was drawn to him and said, "Hey, you ever hit on a ball machine before?" He said, " No sir." "I'm almost finished. You want to hit a few shots on this machine?" "Yes sir." He came out of the fenced training area, around the corner and into my court. I set him up where the balls would be at a successful level, turned on the machine and he began to hit. The balls went everywhere. When the machine emptied, he started to leave. I drew from my experiences and remembered what the great 1920's French tennis player Jean Borotra told me when I received the number one player-in-the-world award at the 1991 ITF World Champion Dinner. He said, "Young man, I don't really know what it is you do, but do it as long as you can." Mr. Borotra was 89 at the time and died the next year. I shared my version of these words with the kid and he said, "Yes sir."

He went back to the backboard and took up hitting again. On the fourth stroke, he hit the ball over the backboard. Embarrassed, he looked around to see if anyone had noticed, put his racket down, trotted around the fence to retrieve the ball, returned and *started over*.

As a tear swelled in my eye, I bonded with the boy. I knew his focus, his determination and his love. And I was reminded *what my next move will always be.*

Who This Book Is For

British Historian Edward Gibbon said, "Even though I am un-provided with original learning, unformed in the habits of thinking, unskilled in the arts of composition, I resolve to write a book." I have been keeping notes for years in the hope of writing, but I always questioned my ability. Epictetus once said, "If you wish to be a writer, you must write," so one day I just started.

As the file on my laptop grew, I was in awe of the amount of work it has taken, the hundreds of times I have labored at my keyboard, reworking sentences, putting myself in the shoes of the reader. Mixed with the moments I thought my work was good against the numerous times I looked at this project and wondered what I was doing…have I finally finished? In reality I don't think a writer ever finishes, I think they just stop writing.

I doubt this will be considered a priceless contribution to the anecdotal literature of the physically challenged, but there is something here for the newly injured, the business executive, a mother of a disabled child and the professional athlete. Reaching extreme peaks and valleys, if anyone has lived in 40 years, I believe I have. An interesting awareness occurred though, as the revisions were taking place. Certainly my ego tells me I have provided wisdom and lessons for many, but in the end, this book is for me.

How This Book Is Organized

Pushing Forward is divided into three sections. The first section is an autobiography "walking" you through my childhood, injury and rehab and then my wheelchair sports career. Filled with anecdotes and antidotes, this section offers insight to the most significant happenings in my life. As an amputee-athlete from Bosnia once told me about his story, "Trust me, it isn't ordinary."

The second section presents some meaningful and illuminating stories encountered *along the way* about finding the point, overcoming adversity and making a stand. No chicken soup here; with lots of meat and spice, this is gumbo.

The third section presents my personal perspective of living life in a wheelchair. It offers confessions from what I call *the paradox*, my injury, which has simultaneously been the best and worst thing to have happened to me.

I've read other writers of this specific type of book like Hockenberry, Wilkins, Callahan and Corbet and enjoyed their prose. The importance of this memoir, though, is that it's from me and written in my style. These are my musings, some famous, others shameful, many of triumph, success and failure, but certainly with my mark. As I made decisions on the entries, I related to Edna St. Vincent Millay who said, "A person who publishes a book willfully appears in public with their pants down." But this book wouldn't have an impact if it weren't true.

SECTION ONE

RANDY SNOW

Chapter
One

> *Nothing in the whole world is permanent. Still waters*
> *never reach the sea.*
> ✳ *Blaze Gaude*

Background

Would I shock you if I told you that I didn't want to be in a wheelchair? If I told you I was initially bitter, would this be a surprise? Permanent injury? To me, permanent was used when talking about the foundation of a house or wedding vows, not about an injury. Permanent meant forever, and profoundly speaking, forever was a long time. No, I wasn't too excited about the word being tossed around. One of the "roll models" at Craig Rehabilitation Hospital, who had been injured forever (I think it was 4 years) gave me some advice that really hurt but had the teeth of truth. He said, "Welcome to the club brother, you are going to be here for awhile."

It is said that if one had a choice of when to incur a permanent disability, it would either be at birth, so he wouldn't know any different, or later in life, so he may have the maturity to accept the situation. Tough luck for me because at sixteen, I landed "smack dab" in the middle. In 1975 my dreams were just evolving. I was developing as an athlete, impressing a few naïve girls and acquiring an illusional, yet semi-functional idea of how life worked. I was beginning to see beyond high school with plans of completing college and pursuing some sort of business career. I was becoming a good tennis player and had hopes of attracting a scholarship to play at the University of Texas.

In reality I had no idea what I was going to do or where I was going to do it. But I was finally beginning to like myself. I was beginning to understand the rules.

Why must we lose something before we truly appreciate it? Damaging my spinal cord derailed the entire plan. All of a sudden, who I was didn't fit into who I was attempting to become. In speaking with others around the world about their initial thoughts after their injuries, I found that there exist many different roads to

4

acceptance. Mine was filled with the fear of living my life in conde-
scension. Being wheelchair-bound held the mark of tragedy, of lost
dreams, of pity, grueling effort and regret. Self-esteem is the most
important ingredient in the recipe of developing as a healthy person. Without belief in oneself, the foundation that a person's life is
being built upon will be unsteady. From my view of what was left,
my self-esteem was being "stomped on."

> *When something gets in your eye, water rushes to the*
> *rescue for temporary relief, but at some time the real*
> *problem must be dealt with.*
> ❋ *Jill Wesson*

Coping Mechanisms

When my accident happened, a plethora of coping mechanisms
surfaced. Some healthy, some not, we all deal with adversity the best
we can. At the time, I didn't even know what a coping mechanism
was, but in retrospect, mine were loud and clear.

It was all about fear. Even today I am largely motivated by fear.
I don't know if it's because I'm stubborn, or an athlete or because
I'm a guy, but fear is a common thread that weaves through me like
a fiber. Perhaps it's a factor for all of us. Back then, in a brand new
body, fear was mighty. Bruce Scott once told me an acronym for fear
is Future Events Appearing Real, which correctly represents those
looming events that most of the time don't hold any truth at all.
Mark Twain said, "I am an old man who has known many worries,
many of which have never happened." Fear just makes things
worse. It robs us of the beauty of the moment. When fear rears its
ugly head, a protection mode of coping mechanisms takes over.

Denial usually pervades first, offering the deception that it isn't
really happening. Caught up in money and "perceived duty," a
shocking example of denial occurs when, after having incurred a
spinal cord injury, a football player is not only applauded as he is
removed from the field but is casually replaced by another player. I
know Michael Irvin of the Dallas Cowboys has not made the best
decisions in his life, but quitting football after incurring a neck injury
and avoiding potential paralysis, established the idea that he still

had some lucidity. Denial, or unwillingness, does have a function though, as it allows us to buy time while preparing for acceptance, if it ever comes.

Then bargaining, the stepsister of denial, can wittingly present "jail house prayers'" as a trade for escape. "I promise God, if you will just…" Next the imposters of depression and anger come to the rescue with the hope of masking the unwelcome hardship. All of these were definitely at my party. They must be experienced and exhausted before acceptance and integration can occur. We must become sick and tired of staying the same or we will not change.

My parents began our family as *normal* as could be expected, whatever *normal* means. In the wheelchair world, the only *normal* we know is a setting on a washing machine. Middle-class suburbia in a small town in the panhandle of Texas, strong family values, recreation and promising future; it was "The Wonder Years." I became athletic, promising, eager and selfish. I began to look forward to the future. Why not, I was just 16 years old.

I had experienced some adversity in my early years. I wet the bed until I was ten, was caught smoking cigarettes behind my house and along with my buddy Steve, stole two checks from his mother, wrote them out for $1.50 with crayons and spent the money on Hot Wheel cars and cotton candy. When my dad found out, he took me out of my third grade class on a "field trip" to the Kaufman County Courthouse. He placed me in each seat of the criminal process including the judge, the plaintiff and the defendant. Now there was some adversity for you.

The first real adversity for me was the morning my parents announced they were not going to be together any longer. At twelve years old, this was devastating. That school day was unforgettable as I distinctly remember having a strong attitude of indifference towards life. Over time we pulled together and as my parents remarried, everyone did some commendable settling. Time has afforded some maturity and I now realize the struggles parents go through when breaking a partnership. Making the difficult move to take care of oneself yet splitting the family unit definitely tests all parties involved, especially in what is right and healthy. It was my first big experience in things not going my way.

But then mach adversity arrived. My stepsister died at the age of fourteen after her body reacted to medication during treatment of an ear infection. The surreptitious struggles of my stepbrother proved too much and at the age of seventeen, he attempted to end his life, then was successful six years later. And I broke my back. My step-siblings' accidents and my injury all happened within a one year period.

Our early family experiences demanded much, yet these events tested our foundation and provided a growing process during the survival, allowing us humility, love, appreciation and gratitude.

Chapter Two

The Accident

I couldn't wait to start school. The baby fat was gone, I could comprehend trigonometry, I was good in sports and I had a beautiful girlfriend. The size of my dreams fit my appetite for life; I was about to be a "star."

With most kids in high school, summer employment was an opportunity to facilitate freedom. My grandfather used to say, "You need a little pocket money." I secured a summer job with a small family business that focused on vehicle servicing and maintenance. My responsibilities were split between running the gas station on the main drag, and when it didn't rain, baling hay. Abhorring the latter, I would much rather have stayed at the station and been involved in the more important work of checking out who was "cruising" Moore Avenue.

When we baled hay, we would load up the equipment before sun-up, then work all day and sweat in some scorching field. My job was to drive a front-end loader and retrieve round bales of hay while Mr. Oakley ran the baler. On July 28, 1975 around 4:30 in the afternoon, I was working in an obscure pasture somewhere near the Texas Oklahoma border. Mr. Oakley had welded six foot metal spikes inside the scoop of the tractor that were positioned under the bales when lifting. I had carried out that same maneuver a thousand times that summer. Using the ungainly front-end loader, I lifted a single 1000-ib. bale with the intention of placing it on a flat bed trailer, but it was giving me trouble. The sheer weight of the bale was pulling the back wheels of the International Harvester tractor off the ground, so I pulled back on the control, asking the hydraulics to raise it a little higher. Raised just above me, the bale dislodged, rolled over the back of the scoop, and landed right on top of me.

Nothing I had done before, or ever could do in life for that matter, would prepare me for that moment. Time froze and accelerated simultaneously as the huge bale fell and crushed me into the steering compartment of the tractor.

I remember overwhelming panic, blackness with streaks of light, and intense pressure. Sandwiched in between the steering wheel and the bale, I attempted to struggle against the monstrous weight but it was futile, as the accident had hurt me badly. I was totally conscience with clear thoughts, yet nothing could be done. The combat moment was surreal.

After the impact, I was in survival shock. I had no idea of the severity of the injury. I struggled for about 30 minutes trying to breathe while attempting to get Mr. Oakley's attention by ineptly honking the horn with my unbroken arm. He finally noticed, stopped the baler, dismounted, and began walking, then running towards me. We were both stunned with urgency. He "shuffled" for a moment, decided, then pulled me off the tractor.

On top of a raincoat, he dragged me to his old car and after pulling out the back seat, lay me into the space. Words can't describe the pain I felt as he lifted me off that tractor and dragged me across that field. I felt like I was being electrocuted through my lower back. My consciousness began to fade. A World War II veteran, Mr. Oakley later told me he had witnessed a great deal of trauma. I still have the letter he wrote, recognizing me for bravery during that time.

We immediately rushed to the community hospital in Paris, TX where they cut off my pants, injected me with morphine, hastily concluded they could do nothing and sent me to St. Paul Hospital in Dallas. Flying in an ambulance Code 3 for several hours on morphine, with parents waiting at strategic places along the highway, is a movie in itself.

The last thing I remember was my father yelling to the ambulance drivers, "I will buy the backboard, just let him go into the hospital." I vaguely remember thinking "What does a backboard have to do with all this?" In the end I had four broken ribs, a compound fracture of my left humerus, a punctured right lung and my twelfth thoracic vertebrae had become extinct.

During 5 hours of surgery, my neurosurgeon attempted to give the damaged area of the spinal cord a chance through a decompression of the crushed spine. He then stabilized the ribs, set up suction for the lung and pinned my broken arm. I didn't find out until later but I was initially diagnosed with a ruptured aorta, which prompted the staff to prepare my family for the possibility of my death.

The next few days were fogged with morphine, dreams and pain. When I finally came to, I vaguely heard the sound of counting "1-2-3" and in pain, I was spun from face up to face down. I was now on a Striker bed, which displaced my weight to discourage pressure sores. They would press me between two pieces of canvass surrounded by a metal frame and "rotate" me every two hours. Periodic morphine and recurrent dreams, regular rotation and drifting pairs of relatives, made the following days imaginary.

In hope of cheering me up, someone hung a *Garfield* cat behind my bed. Though only twelve inches tall, on morphine he appeared twelve feet tall. Thinking the grinning was an indication that I was about to be eaten, for about twenty minutes, I had to defend myself against a quite convincing tiger.

The morphine was awful. The dreams were hallucinatory and potent. I recall my dad and I putting off the injections, adding five minutes at a time until I didn't need them anymore. And my mom, step-dad, Aunt Harriet and my sisters placing their lives on hold and living at a nearby hotel for two months, not really knowing what to do next. My family deserves recognition for their patience to have answered so many inquiries about my status. I can only imagine what my parents thought during the ordeal. I vicariously lived through the stories of what they were doing and welcomed the reports. "What ifs" were amplified and depressing.

I was eventually transferred out of intensive care to a single room on the seventh floor. More cards and visitors, lots of pain, hospital food and speculation...what was going to happen? We had all seen enough of this on television; everyone walked away from this kind of accident. I was an athlete who had experienced many injuries, and I had overcome them all. I *knew* I would overcome this as well.

My doctor eventually had "the talk" with my parents. Doctors—they always portray the worst scenario, I suppose they must. He said the accident had left me permanently paralyzed from the waist down. The prognosis included dependence, pressure sores, inactivity and sympathy. They tried to explain to me that I would never walk again, but when *permanent* was mentioned, inside I recoiled like a hot flame. I felt like I was somebody else.

What had I used to qualify my life prior to my injury? Everything that I had loved to do as enjoyable and rewarding was gone. Walking through the woods, hunting and fishing, running to the net to shake my opponent's hand, a cramp in my hamstring, the feel of new blue-jeans on the first day of school, water skiing...my freedom, my future...all of it was gone. With the weight of an elephant, a feeling of "this can't be happening" stood on me. In private all I could do was cry. But AHHH...denial, the trusty defender of our inner child. I told myself, not me, I am different, I am going to walk,

I don't need to listen, this is all fine for "you people" but I don't plan on being like this for very long.

What to Do?

Experiencing paralysis is puzzling because the area you can't feel is considered foreign, yet it's still attached. You are two people. The accident is so close to who you were, your mind has difficulty sorting it out. For me, there was no immediate adjustment, only denial.

Once I remember being lost for what seemed like hours while a nurse gave my legs a sponge bath. Not being able to feel the wash cloth, I wondered about sensory nerves and synapses, about how quick the messages used to travel through my legs to my brain. An experiment for you; lightly touch the page of this book with your finger and become aware of how fast the message travels along your arm, your brain ascertains the source of the touch and determines it's safety. The effectiveness and efficiency of the human body is amazing.

At such a young age, I really didn't have anyone or anything tangible to receive my anger. Who could I be mad at? My coping skills for this type of experience weren't grounded. You have to start over after a spinal cord injury and learn to do things as an infant might. I had returned to being naked most of the time, peeing and pooping on myself, unsure and dependent on people for everything. As an athlete before my injury, my new body offended me. The voice of doubt was taking advantage and saying, "You're paralyzed, you can't do this, give in, let others take care of you, you aren't worth it, kill yourself."

My family was fortunate to have the resources that allowed research of rehabilitation facilities around the world and the decision was made to transfer me to Craig Rehabilitation Institute in Englewood, Colorado. We were told that in 90 days I would be dressing, driving and independent in personal hygiene, so Craig would be the womb where I would redevelop my life. At sixteen years old, I would start over.

Not that my real dad or mom weren't problem solvers, but the "at arm's length" of my stepfather's newness in the family desensitized the necessary process of making decisions. Love sometimes freezes the right move. Thank God he was there because nothing was "buttered." He would meet with the doctors, get the information and steer us in what seemed to be the best decision and *push forward*. There wasn't a lot of time to dwell on things. We were always *pushing forward*.

The flight to Denver provided me with an idea of future humility. The airline had removed the seats in first class where they had set my gurney. I received an early initiation of people "gawking" as each passenger came around the corner of the plane to see me lying on my back under a sheet. No question about it, I was the most unusual flight attendant on board. And if that wasn't enough humility, upon our arrival the staff decided to take me down the steps and out the back. As soon as we descended to the runway, a big wind came up and blew my sheet off the gurney, exposing me to everyone looking down through the windows. Thinking on my…back…I just waved.

Craig Hospital

Rehab was a plethora of challenges, a focus group of life with people in different circumstances and varying resources. Inhibition and privacy were nonexistent; we didn't have the luxury of secrets. It was like a tornado came through the neighborhood, then after the storm, every one came out of their home to see what kind of damage was done. Some were totally destroyed while the house next door may have only lost a shingle. Everyone looked around to see how he faired against the others.

Muscle was as precious as gold. It was a humbling feeling to lay in a hospital bed attempting to move a muscle that just wasn't there. Even a trace muscle could bring joy to the face of a spinal cord victim. I could twitch my left quadricep and thought because of this, I was going to walk. It was this *hope* that kept me coming to therapy. Many were worse off while some had much more *return*. Some couldn't cut up their own food while others had cranberry juice, the worst drink known to a sixteen-year old kid, *encouraged* down their throats.

Return was a euphemism with many meanings. It ostensibly referred to the sensation or muscle that sometimes *returns* after paralysis. Lucky ones had huge amounts of *return* that allowed them to walk the halls, while others consistently prayed for it at night. As with the characters in the book *Girl, Interrupted*, *return* also represented the idea that someday we would *return* back to our homes, our friends and our lives. Finally, *return* symbolized our true dream, what all of us really wanted to do; just *return* to the person we were before our injury. We all lived for *return*.

The first day in the physical therapy gym was shocking. Upon arrival, I was quickly educated as to the various types of injuries. Some were young and had severe neck injuries, with a few on an artificial breathing apparatus. Others were older individuals whose lives had been displaced by the devastation of a stroke. Diabetes patients with recent amputations and "fresh" head injuries were there as well. It was a shantytown of trauma and hope, of which I truly wanted no part. I did not belong there.

Without much success, I attempted to run the show using sympathy, as I had done in my acute setting, but it quickly became apparent that I wasn't in charge. I had decided to spend the first few days in my room but my therapist, Beverly, had other plans. She unplugged my bed and moved the entire unit down the hall. Wishing I was invisible, I just lay there in the physical therapy gym.

Time *softened* my non-compliant attitude though, and I began to settle in. The first thing I attempted to achieve in rehabilitation was independent catheterization. There wasn't much dignity in a stranger pulling down my pants every couple of hours, sloshing Betadine around and sticking a tube in my penis. Being able to cath on my own was a milestone. The second item of desired liberty was to do the bowel program independently. This necessary task was hard to accept not only from the physical demands but psychologically as well. Gloved or not, as long as I could remember, I had never touched my own excrements, but my mother reminded me that at a much earlier age, both of us had touched it often. The bowel program was a dreaded chore.

Dressing myself and making my own chair transfers offered additional fragments of freedom. Learning how to get dressed, for the second time, which now took me around an hour, was a huge turning point. Putting pants on paralyzed legs was like putting on wet socks times a hundred. In order to get dressed independently, all of us had our families bring the easiest clothes we could think of, as our entire wardrobes consisted of cotton sweats. I could barely reach my feet, much less put on a sock, but every day, *pushing forward* got easier and easier. I still remember making my first transfer off the lobby couch to my wheelchair. Similar to the elation of when I finally learned how to pop a "wheelie," I couldn't wait to tell everybody at lunch. Those daily living skills took hours of practice, but considering the tasks some of the others were attempting, my successes were top shelf events.

Overall the environment was a psychological war zone. Cathing myself after an hour transfer to a toilet or watching my legs float in the pool as if they were drifting in space fed my escapism. To this day, the *memory* of working on daily living skills still demands my attention. We just blindly *pushed forward*, following the direction of our "field generals" as none of us had any real choice in the matter. We did rehab one-minute-at-a-time as we searched for hidden pieces of progress.

If Only I Had a Little More

> *If we compare, we will always be vain or bitter because there is always someone worse off or better off than us.*
> ✳ *Paralympic tennis player, Sharon Clark*

When it's difficult, when life changes, when we aren't getting what we think we deserve, there is a tendency to compare. In hope of minimizing the situation, some of us compare to people who are worse off and think we have it made. Occasionally though we compare to people who are better off and think we would be OK if we were in their situation. It's easy to look back at our lives and offer statements like, "If only I had done this…" or "I wish I was like them." The most common comment in rehab was, "I wish I had a little more."

Within the struggle of rehab, my comparison led me to a guy named Skip. He could wheel, dress and transfer by himself. He was the successful businessman, the perfect family, the star athlete. I wished I had what he had. When we went on outings around the block, which seemed like a million miles, he always finished first. Each day as we would meet at the drive, I would say to myself, "If only I could push like Skip, I would be OK." The recreational therapist would send us out and I would be on Skip's wheels, but as he got to the first corner, he would start up the hill and disappear. He was good in his chair. There were about sixty other patients who physically had less, but I chose to compare myself to the one guy who had more.

One might think this standard might have motivated me to successfully complete my treatment plan. I know this isn't true. More often than not, the *tendency* in life is to dwell on what we don't have. This weighs us down with expectations that are based on another's situation. Distracting us from the task at hand, comparison draws our attention away from our strengths. I hadn't compared to Skip for motivation. I was comparing my situation to his because I wanted to be miserable. My comparison made me angry and envious.

Chapter Three

> *It is more painful to stay the same than it is to change.*
> ✳ *Harriet Lee Gunder*

Competing

Recognizing my struggles, Beverly challenged me to a new perspective. Therapists are very special people. When we arrive at rehab, we are not only stripped of our physical abilities, we also come psychologically, emotionally and spiritually bankrupt. We are like soft-shell crabs after abandoning our shell in a threatening ocean, looking for another home. She knew I was having a difficult time and knew what to say. She met me one morning in my room as I was preparing for the day and left me with some very important wisdom. Beverly said, "Listen, I am not in your shoes. I know this is hard, but I want you to focus on answering three questions. First, a positive *attitude* is a must. Forget the past and let go of the future. Leave everything you have on the mats. What will your *attitude* be? Secondly, you have so much left, be *accountable* by taking action, by focusing on your strengths. Stop comparing to the people around you and especially to Skip. You are different people with different minds and bodies. Where will you be *accountable*? And with the best of your ability, problem solve each day. How will you *adapt*? Be a competitor. Competing will not make your life wonderful, but it will make it possible."

Due to the injury and the following *atrophy* to my arm, initially I had a hard time pushing my wheelchair. *Atrophy* is another word in rehab that demands respect because muscle has amnesia. It's amazing how fast it falls off the bone. After just 5 weeks of immobilization, I could not lift my arm off my chest. I could either raise my elbow or my hand, but I couldn't lift them both at the same time. I would struggle down the hall to breakfast and then to mat class. I was always late.

The first time I began to compete was when I decided to improve my punctuality at morning mat class. Juan, a quadriplegic, roomed next door to me and used a power chair. They were called electric wheelchairs back then and I was pretty sure I didn't *deserve* one of them. Each day he would whiz by me on his way to class, beating me by minutes. We are only talking about fifty feet. One day, I noticed he had little handles on the back of his power wheelchair. I thought if I could only hold on to those handles, he could pull me to class. That night I presented the idea to Juan, who said, "No problemo."

The next morning I could hear his power chair coming down the hall towards my room. Stopping in front of my door, he let me get a hold, said "Vamonos" and we were on our way. We started down the hall, went around the corner, past the nurse's station and stopped just outside the doors of the physical therapy gym. Allowing Juan to go first, I followed through the doors into the gym. Surprised, Beverly said, "I am very proud of you, did you push all the way down to the gym?" Knowing the sooner I finished the requirements of the treatment plan I would get to go home, that being punctual to all meetings and classes were items on that list, and being a normal teenager, I said, "Yes ma'am." This secret "piggybacking" went on for four days, with rave support from my treatment team.

One morning, as Juan and I were cruising down the hall, my footrest began to rub on Juan's 20-inch rear tire. The sharp edges of my footplates pinched the tire, which grabbed my front end and suddenly flipped me over on my back. I was quickly reminded that paralysis and gravity work great together, because both my knees struck me right in the nose. Lying on the floor with watering eyes in an upside down wheelchair, I was barely able to see Juan disappear into the cafeteria, as the "commitment of his joystick" never wavered.

This was not what Beverly meant when she said be a competitor, but her advice was sound. As I began to let my guard down, have fun and try new things, the change had begun.

The fight within comes from the foundation of our being, and must be accessed by the individual.
✳ *Errol Marklein, German gold medalist,*
1988 Paralympics in Korea

Discharge

Discharge nowadays is the day the insurance company says there isn't any more money. In 1975, discharge was the day the "team" reached a consensus that the patient's daily living skills had attained a healthy level of sufficiency that warranted a safe return home.

To properly capture the emotions on this day, I'll ask you to re-visit your early childhood, say three years old. As your friends surround you on a hot summer day, all of you are splashing away in the baby pool. Remember the comfort of the shallow water, how safe you felt with your friends and family, and even in the middle, you could put your feet right on the bottom. If you did happen to slip, someone would quickly be at your side to rescue you from the threatening situation.

Then one day the swim instructor makes a very shocking an-nouncement. "Today will be our first day in the big pool." As those words are spoken, you glance in the direction of the thing your mother had warned was dangerous, as a nervous feeling begins to flow through your veins. As you walk up to the edge and peer into that deep blue abyss, fear overwhelms. You knew this day would come and you are overcome with emotion.

The day we return home is very similar. Arriving at rehab un-sure, we slowly developed skill and confidence, only to leave a very safe environment to return to the world that sent us there in the first place. But the fact that we were injured there was not the key issue, rather, we returned somebody completely different. After their first child was born, my sister and her husband walked into their house knowing the situation was supposed to be wonderful yet *they could-n't breathe*. The training at the hospital was valuable, but nothing could have truly prepared them for that moment. They left as one unit and returned a completely different family. Similarly, returning is a very contradicting day in our lives. Any feelings of celebration and accomplishment are accompanied by the fear of leaving our supportive surroundings. Attempting to fly for the very first time, I assure you an eaglet has difficulty drawing a breath as it looks over the edge of the nest.

Mistakes were encouraged and accepted at Craig. If one couldn't successfully transfer back into their wheelchair after a floor transfer, there was always a safety net. But at home, daily living skills and transfers were solo. We all knew discharge was right but it didn't reduce our anxiety.

I remember the day Skip was discharged. He exhibited confidence and happiness but underneath, I knew he was afraid. Like going from the baby pool to the big pool, college to the work force, dating to marriage, track practice to the Olympics, drug treatment to an A.A. meeting; he was on his way to the real world. He reminded me of a Spanish explorer who had convinced the King that the world was round with treasures waiting to be discovered. Surviving the scrutiny, he would be encouraged to pursue and realize these treasures, all the time wondering if he had made a mistake by buying into the progressive thinking of the minority.

Then, one day he was just gone. He never called, never wrote, he sent no messages, there was no contact. We never saw him again. Down by the flagpole, where the informal support groups occurred, our fears about discharge and home were confirmed, the world really was *flat*. Discharge was fearfully anticipated.

Born on the 4th of July

Home still held mystical power as I thought I would be OK if I could just get there. Residing in a small town made my return home ceremonious. They were all there, they all came…there he is…welcome back…what's it like? My arrival was correctly portrayed in the movie *Born On The 4th Of July* when, thinking he was returning to the world he left, Tom Cruise really arrived in a foreign place.

Everyone in my hometown anticipated my return, yet no one, including myself, had any idea of what to do. With more innocence than pity, my hometown embraced me, and even though I was the same person, a lot of my acquaintances had changed. Many of the students and teachers in my high school were not able to face what turned out to be their own pain or handicaps. It was like my personality was attached to my legs.

Some of my friends made huge attempts to be close. One guy got a little too close. Like an open window to boys in a third grade class, my girlfriend drew their attention. One night I called one of her admirers into my car. As he sat in the passenger seat of my 1976 Cutlass, I distracted him by pointing away, and as he looked, I "sucker punched" him across the bridge of his nose. Trust me, fighting an able-bodied guy without the use of your legs is asking for trouble. The next thing I knew, I was on the ground outside my car, on the passenger side, having the living daylights beaten out of me. I definitely appreciated the anaesthetizing effect of the beer in my blood at the time. A rite of passage had occurred though, because my wounds let everyone know that "I wasn't fragile." High school was still a difficult place to make a re-entry.

> *On a certain level I knew I was not comfortable being seen in the world as having a disability. I wanted to appear as normal as possible, perhaps understandably because I had eighteen years of nondisabled identity still inside me.*
> ✳ *Gary Karp*

In retrospect, my misery must have been awful. During the first year after my discharge, in desperation I went to a faith healer. I actually went into a congregation of 800 people as they called the afflicted up onto the stage *to be healed*. I quietly positioned myself in the rear of the church, stayed for a moment, then left in disgust. I was disappointed not only because I knew the whole act was misleading but because my inability to accept my situation allowed me to believe that I actually might come home, walk in the door and announce, "Look, God healed me, it's all OK now." This testifies to the level of my denial and how much I loathed being in a wheelchair.

Like a first generation Japanese female living in America, I didn't fit in either world. My mind could still walk but my body couldn't. I was surrounded by people, family, medical staff, and old and new friends, yet I was totally alone. In an attempt to find something I could do, artist Helon Thompson introduced me to oil painting, and though I learned a great deal about burnt sienna and my light source, it wasn't who I was. To this day, I appreciate her effort and still keep those paintings in my home to remember that time.

My refusal to accept lingered for three years after my injury. I distinctly remember avoiding other people in wheelchairs, crossing the street as they approached me on the sidewalk. Figuratively speaking, I can empathize with the pain a closet gay person may feel. I remember the first time I attended a wheelchair basketball game. I just sat there in the corner hoping *they* wouldn't talk to me. Naturally one of the players came over and asked if I wanted to play. I recall seeing a videotape of the great David Kiley reminiscing about the time just after he was injured and saying, "I am a basketball player, I don't play in a wheelchair." This was exactly how I felt.

My tennis friends would come over to visit, then go out on our tennis court to play. I would not go with them and cried as I watched them through the window. With reservation, I remember strolling out and attempting to hit against the backboard. Just in case it was fun or if I failed, I did it in private because I didn't want anybody to see me doing either. Although feeling the ball on the strings again felt great, I remember coming up with all kinds of excuses why it wouldn't work. Maybe it was because if I participated and had fun, then I really was in a wheelchair.

Chapter
Four

Still Me

In the movies, the handicapped guy finds himself in some quiet, thought-filled melodramatic moment when he sees the "burning bush." Surrounded by the music of John Williams, the enlightenment of Ghandi and the bravado of Rocky, he realizes what must be done. He is overwhelmed with wisdom and enthusiasm with his decision, and in one great swoop, he willingly accepts the challenge and joins his destiny.

This wasn't the case for me. The *redefinition* of the important aspects of living was not overnight. It took me a long time to settle in and welcome the permanent fact that I wouldn't be able to use my legs. The acceptance and integration of my accident was, and is, a perpetual process void of ceremony. My "I've had enough" mechanism still responds slowly. There is only one *acceptance road*, but there are many different speeds. Trite as it sounds, consciously knowing we have *worth* is key.

The real connection was the awareness that I was "still me." Expressed in the title of the memoir written by Christopher Reeve, even though my mobility base had changed and most of society now looked upon me differently, I was still me. I was Randy Snow. I still liked sports, enjoyed the outdoors, being the center of attention, laughing, sunshine, people and the world. Of course I wished my accident had not happened, but if I was true to myself, not only could I accept my spinal cord injury, I could handle anything life might deliver. My new challenge was to get back to the things I loved.

Comfort Zones

By 1978, I had only been in my new body a few years and was slowly becoming more independent, but I was still very unsure. The transition from able-bodied to disabled male is difficult in Texas because the nonsense of not being able to "fix a fence post" can present a stigma of inadequacy. More a perception than reality, the adage "can't carry, can't contribute," can linger. When we discover a method of mowing the lawn for example, or carrying out the trash, we are very pleased. It isn't the act that pleases, but the *adaptation of the execution* that has value. Something as simple as getting dressed in your wheelchair can bring unbelievable rewards.

Whether you believe in sport hunting or not, this story is significant to me. For many years my idea of hunting took on more of a conservative view, but today I hold high regard for being in the wild, appreciating the "gift" as the Lipan Apaches before me. The Texas hill country *appears* unfriendly and barren, with lots of rocks, cactus and mesquite trees, but to me, the areas surrounding San Antonio are rich in indigenous foliage and history. From annual Thanksgiving weekends to frequent trips for all kinds of reasons, I have developed a deep love for the hill country and can thank my step-father Tom Norton, who has visited the area since he was a child, for introducing me to this magical region.

I had completed the first phases of rehab and was attending classes at the University of Texas. My parent's ranch wasn't far from Austin, where our family recreated, hunted and fished. Currently it is used more for the rekindling of our souls and family recharging, but years ago my stepfather annually leased hunting property in the area for entertaining clients.

Opening day was reserved for the men, a "testosterone weekend" of food, hunting and "telling lies." That morning we loaded up into "Old Blue" and headed out to our blinds. The "oil well blind" was where I would hunt and was the first drop. After getting my chair out of the vehicle, the guys set it up where I could easily transfer and I began gathering my gear. The terrain in the hill country of Texas is extremely rocky, which makes it difficult to maneuver. I took my time in the dark, deftly popping wheelies and balancing my chair. Transferring into the seat, I let the light, then the sound of their vehicle, disappear. Being alone in the wild activates the senses algebraically. The silence in the dark is deafening. Sometimes a cry or a grunt may be heard with no known origin of the animal existing in your brain. I was aware that I wouldn't see them for hours.

The first rays of the sun arrived and against the backdrop of a draw, I could barely make out the silhouette of a deer. As more light arrived, I was able to "put horns" on this deer and my pulse quickened. Though I had full intention of taking an animal, the reality was, I had not hunted alone since my injury. If I were to take this animal, how would I physically carry out the responsibility of processing it? In order to save the meat, this must be done immediately. My trepidation was quickly replaced by "buck fever," so I sighted in, relaxed and pulled the trigger. As I wheeled towards the downed deer I was filled with questions. I had processed many deer before, but had never carried it out from a chair. What would have ordinarily taken me 20 tidy minutes was finished in an untidy hour and a half. It was extremely difficult but I did it. Beaming, I transferred back into my chair and proudly wheeled back to my blind.

It was the growth over the next couple of hours that was significant. Because I was able to execute and complete this difficult task, in private without the subjection of public failure, the likelihood of the attempt and development of my confidence was significantly enhanced. If I had not wanted to fit in, to be a part of a group, I would not have taken the risk. Sometimes this can be a significant issue for people who live their life from a wheelchair. Having to prove oneself can detrimentally loom.

The story reminds me of the time I was coaching at a junior wheelchair basketball camp in Dallas. Circumstance placed a player named Richard on a scrimmage team with older players. Michael, one of the more advanced players, had attempted to pass the ball to Richard, which resulted in failure. I overheard the other kids saying "No, no, don't pass it to him." They even slacked their defense on him. Conscious of the compensatory act, Richard badly wanted to be accepted as a contributing player on the team. The situation presented itself again, and against the suggestions of his teammates, Michael passed Richard the ball. This was it; he wasn't going to fail. Richard opened his arms wide letting the basketball hit him full in the stomach, which knocked the wind out of him. To the amazement of the other kids, he gathered himself, then passed the ball back to Michael, who scored a basket. Gasping for air while wheeling back down the court, he glanced into the stands at his mother who clapped approvingly.

> *You can put all the pieces of the puzzle out there on the table, but they have to do it themselves.*
> ✳ *Marcha Moore, coach of the Women's 1993 World Team Cup champions*

According to water-skiing accident victim and professional speaker Skip Wilkins, it's about shifting the focus from *what* has happened, to *how* am I going to deal with it. Understandably in my early days, I was focusing on what I had lost. But when I began to compete, I began to look at my situation with the problem solving of a challenger. Disregarding the past and future, focusing on strengths and adapting became my principles. Giving it a little time, I began to *recreate my dreams.* Venturing out of my comfort zones and competing with myself reduced the pressure of meeting unrealistic expectations and magnified my focus on the immediate solution.

> *Change is permanent, who we are is not.*
> ✳ *Mary Allison Snow*

Compete Platforms: How Do We Compete?

Entrepreneur and Minnesota Vikings owner, Red McCombs once said, "From the receptionist to the franchise player, if we aren't improving we are getting worse." I believe this is true; we are either competing or dying, there is no middle ground. The following Compete Platforms are compulsory to the process of overcoming any adversity and I share them with companies, associations and schools around the world.

Compete Platform #1   ATTITUDE
Am I based in the moment?

Said a million different ways, it's all about *Attitude*. Our *Attitude* is the perfect medication; it will make us unbreakable. During change, there is a tendency to want it the way it was or to worry about the way it is going to be. Worrying about either distracts us from the moment. Staying in the moment guarantees a healthy *Attitude* that will positively affect our ability to handle any situation. This doesn't mean neglect making plans, rather understand the difference between *expectations* and *aspirations*. Just like choosing a good pair of underwear, what kind of *attitude* will I choose today?

Compete Platform #2   ACCOUNTABILITY
What will I do about the situation?

Regardless of who is at fault, when we become *Accountable*, it means we are willing to do something about our situation. Being *Accountable* is about options. Options invite a willingness to take action. I read about a lady who attempted to commit suicide. She said she just ran out of options. If we play the victim, our destiny is left up to someone else. Life is full of blame. I pity athletes that are blamers and complainers. If we are willing to take action, we assume ownership of our destiny and *push forward*. What are my strengths?

Compete Platform #3   ADAPTABILITY
Will I adapt?

Without a doubt, life promises to change our resources, interests, priorities and challenges. True leaders achieve success with available resources. Our ability to *Adapt* to the situation is paramount. New ways of thinking, problem solving, and obstacle-handling techniques (OHTs) are a must when overcoming challenges. Am I a problem solver?

Leadership today suggests change on the inside is lasting. Rather than doing kind things, we must become kind people. If our motives are healthy, our principles in place and our processes true, the outcomes we seek will find us. We won't need to pursue them.

In the movie based on James Fenimore Cooper's classic book, *Last of the Mohicans*, Hawkeye, played by Daniel Day-Lewis, is about to be separated from Madeline Stowe by a group of determined Huron Indians for an indefinite amount of time. Notwithstanding the real reason Day-Lewis aspired to rendezvous with Stowe, with his words he correctly captures what it takes to survive change. In a love-struck yet sternly appropriate tone, Day-Lewis says to Stowe, "You stay alive, no matter what, you stay alive." Surviving adversity teaches us that life goes on. With attitude, accountability and adaptability, we become competitors and can survive anything that comes our way.

> *Sometimes we just have to give ourselves permission to be well.*
> ✳ *U.S.A. men's wheelchair tennis coach Dan James*

Chapter
Five

Family

A combination of factors positively influenced my rehabilitation, but the most invaluable resource of all was the faith and support of my family. It is said, fear cannot exist where there is faith. They had faith in me and I could not let them down. During my four-month rehab, my father called me every single day. My family was at the core of my acceptance. A building is subject to all kinds of elements and can withstand any adversity, if it has a strong foundation. As human beings we also need this foundation, this bulwark. I couldn't ever imagine telling my family that it was too hard or that I couldn't do it. Having them for support, to talk to and to share the pain with, made a huge impact during the early stages.

Inversely speaking, love can dangerously enable, as it filters what's real, causing us to do things we think is best, but in reality are detrimental. The family members who are the hardest on us are actually the ones who love us the most.

At times it's harder for the family. Once Jim Martinson and I went to visit our good friend Wayne, who was in Craig Hospital recovering from a severe accident. After contracting transverse myelitis at an early age, Wayne had lived most of his life from a wheelchair. He had worked in the wheelchair manufacturing industry for many years, traveling the world, and had seemingly seen it all. After a wheelchair sales show in southern California, a maid entered his room and found him lying face down on the floor. He had been there for several hours after having a stroke. Compassion in its purest form might say, "Hey, one debilitating injury per person is enough," but God saw it differently.

Personally I believe these things happen to affect the people surrounding the victim, to continue the growth of their patience and gratitude. Surviving an injury doesn't necessarily mean regaining equivalent function, it means being able to accept situations and again find quality of life.

Sharing our nervousness with each other, we wondered why we held such apprehension. We had frequently been around people involved in accidents but here, we were more uncomfortable than usual. Jim said, "I guess it's harder for the family because they can't do anything about it. It has to be done by the one in the hardship." Our difficulty that day wasn't about watching just anyone experience pain. It was about not being able to *do anything* to help our friend. Without my family, accepting my injury would have been much more difficult.

This section is dedicated to Jim's son, Justin, and Wayne.

Justin passed away during the writing of Pushing Forward *after a traumatic car crash. Upon receiving the news of Justin's passing, in an extremely difficult phone call, Jim contacted a friend on dialysis, to offer his son's kidney in relief. Loved by everyone who knew him, Justin was a very special man.*

Well into the rehab of his stroke, Wayne contracted pneumonia and was placed on a respirator. After miserable conditions and futile attempts to find quality of life, he instructed the hospital staff to disconnect the device. He lived three more days before succumbing to the complications of the stroke.

Do you want to hear God laugh? Tell him your plans.
✳ *Dickie Schilhab*

Our Dreams

Dreams make everyday life tolerable. In school speeches, I tell kids to dream big. Without dreams life would be mediocre. My early dreams had nothing to do with overcoming a spinal cord injury, wheelchair sports or a speaking career. They were filled with playing tennis like Jimmy Conners and winning the U.S. Open. I dreamed of being successful in business, traveling around the world and being surrounded by kids. Initially, my spinal cord injury dashed any hope of achieving those dreams. It's frustrating when the expectations we place on our lives aren't met.

But *re-dreaming* is necessary. As I reflect on the past twenty-five years, I now know that my childhood dreams were realized. Not only did I win the U.S. Open, I won it ten times. I just happened to win it in a wheelchair. I have been very successful, having plenty of money and my travel dreams have been achieved as I have definitely "surfed the earth." The only problem with frequent flyer miles is you have to get on another plane to use them. And lastly, I have 5 younger sisters so every time I go home, there is another niece or nephew that I look forward to introducing myself to (obvious exaggeration), as I am surrounded by children. All my early dreams came true, just not along the path that I had planned.

> *Does the doctor do the healing, does the farmer do the growing, do we really control our lives?*
> ✳ *Rebecca Bowen Rangel*

A New Perspective

I was driving in the small lake community of Heath, Texas (where I lived several years ago) and came upon an intersection that I had previously crossed hundreds of times, either on my hand-cycle or in my car. As I approached, I observed a new four way stop sign at the corner. I thought of the intersection before the stop sign, and how it had seemed just fine the way it was. Now people passing by this junction would have to adjust their busy lives, break their routine and be more aware of their surroundings. For reasons presumed yet not fully known, some form of a Higher Power (the City of Heath) placed this obstacle in the path of passing people.

Slowing my car, I noticed a beautiful old farmhouse with a red barn, and horses and goats in an accompanying pasture. As I stopped, our family friend, Mr. Stephens, was coming the other way and had also stopped. He offered a friendly Texas wave.

Continuing on to my parent's house, it dawned on me that this four way stop sign was a metaphor for my accident. Originally a huge inconvenience and continuously questioned, it helped me realize that God intended for me to slow down, learn something new and have a completely different perspective than before. My accident was placed in my life by my Higher Power for the purpose of seeing through different lenses. In fact these lenses were even turned around so I could have a completely new perspective of my self, that was previously unavailable from the way I was living.

Sometimes when events happen in our life, we superficially acknowledge, criticize the inconvenience, hastily question why and move on. Stuck in an old mindset, this event may provide a new way of looking at life that was unappreciated before. This perspective may even protect us from something life-threatening.

It was written in some scriptorium long ago that after closing one door, God opens another. The problem is this door may not be open yet. It may not even be a door at all, but a window hidden behind some curtains. In fact, this window may not even be in the same house. But these *openings* will be there. One must work a little harder to discover them. Small hidden doors open into large glorious rooms. Had I not experienced my accident I never would have really lived, seen what I have seen, nor met the wonderful people I have met. I never would have developed the necessary process it takes to absorb, adapt and move on. My accident made me a human being rather than a human doing.

> *Miracles do happen, the impossible just takes*
> *a little longer.*
> ✳ *Art Berg*

Chapter Six

> *Sports doesn't build character, it reveals it.*
> ✳ *U.S.A. basketball coach Frank T. Burns*

The Trojan Horse

Unfortunately for most, wheelchair sports is regarded as either a watered-down form of admirable competition or a "feel good" pacifier. It's considered good for *those people*. Even the highest platform, the Olympics, has passed over real recognition and avoided accrediting the exhibition wheelchair races, which debuted in 1984, as full medal sports. Instead, they have acknowledged *infants* like trampoline and beach volleyball, blessing them with Olympic status ahead of the athleticism of Scot Hollenbeck and Candace Cable.

To us, and especially for the ones who have witnessed its development over the years, it carries a much greater value. Due to the nature of my active past, I experienced the extreme contrast of being athletic and independent to full-blown sympathy. Finding a way out of this sympathy brought great value to the *mechanism* that freed me from the imprisonment. Sports created a pathway out of the "condescending corner" and guided me through the prism of dependence. It held my attention like a kite in a twenty-mph wind and I wasn't letting go.

When I had finally reached an acceptance level that allowed sports in, it was finding competition again that motivated me. I will never forget the excitement I felt as I drove to Houston to participate in a track meet that was conducted by the Southwest Wheelchair Athletic Association. And our High Roller Wheelchair Basketball Team rivalries with Will Clark's Houston Rolling Cougars were revered. To have people tell me again that they were impressed with my athleticism tapped into my *passion* and created energy that has stayed with me to this day.

Caution must be considered here as sometimes the wheelchair athlete can run too quickly to sports, using it as a *crutch to avoid feeling*. Existing comfortably around similar people, it can be easy to choose friends that understand the situation, deferring personal growth. The absorption of the change in our life must be complete.

Conversely, of all the disabled individuals I have known over the years, the ones who participate in sport, or at least stay active, have the highest chance of rejoining society, finding work, staying healthy and approaching the life expectancy of our able-bodied counterparts. We need balanced diversity.

Wheelchair sports are extremely competitive. It isn't for the people who need it; it's for the people who want it. To hear a group of racers in the hunt for a purse of $25,000, discuss the next athlete to be left from the pack by a series of surges, isn't feel-good athletics. Or to hear basketball players in the huddle during a national championship game identify a player on the other team, who will be exploited because he is more paralyzed, isn't the Special Olympics. There is no "Pollyanna" attitude in wheelchair sports, but there does exist simultaneous camaraderie and pedigree competition.

Through participation, athletes exercise their option to make choices. These choices define a person as an active participant in their community. From simple community involvement to the glory of the Paralympics, a person who chooses to lead an active lifestyle is breaking down attitudinal barriers, creating avenues for change, in all settings. It is our responsibility to positively affect the world with the skills that have been provided us. As a result of this movement, persons with disabilities have gained equal opportunity and access to a broad range of recreational and sports activities, from neighborhood playgrounds to Paralympic competitions.

This morning I read in *USA Today* that for the first time in history there will be an African-American swimmer, Anthony Irvin, on the U.S.A. swim team going to Sydney. What a wonderful opportunity to be able to change stereotypes in sport and in life. The physically challenged also have this opportunity. Through a demonstrating fashion, disabled athletes educate. Accompanying our sports movement is an educational goal of making individuals say, "I didn't know that." By the way, Anthony Irvin eventually won a gold medal in the 50 free.

> *Advocacy is advocacy.*
> ✳ *International Paralympic Committee member*
> *Duncan Wyeth*

Wheelchair sports invade us like a Trojan Horse. As we tend to build walls to protect our inner child, especially after an accident, sports enters the "mental system." Once inside, the wounds we were guarding are exposed and healed. Life domains are enhanced and opportunities for growth are revealed. The following life domains are specifically affected by participation in wheelchair sports.

- *Physical*—A key to longevity is enhanced circulation. By staying active, weight is kept at a minimum, which helps digestion, respiration, muscular development, transfers and all aspects of life. For example, a quadriplegic that dreams of working a 40-hour week, getting married and raising children can't let his body go. It is unfair for him to ask his wife to help with transfers or his bowel program when he could independently carry out these tasks himself. If this happens, the chances of a healthy relationship are less than average. A healthy body is achieved through sport.

- *Social*—I learned much from traveling, especially overseas. Mark Twain said, "travel is the antithesis of bigotry and discrimination." Realizing we live in a small corner of the world is truly a benefit of globetrotting. Shortcuts are learned from others that have "been there." Especially for the newly injured, observing someone deal with inaccessible rest rooms in Europe or how to transfer to a chair on a slope is invaluable. Sports facilitate social interaction. The luxury of inefficiency is quickly replaced by supreme resourcefulness.

- *Psychological*—It's difficult to accept an injured body after a permanent accident. Sports aid in the development of a healthy body image, contributing to the assertiveness of the individual and the acceptance of self. Attempting a half-marathon challenges the ability of a wheelchair racer in many areas but the self-esteem gained from taking the risk is paramount. A person with a disability must re-develop pride and fill confidence gaps. Sports fill those gaps and teach us to problem solve, efficiently utilize resources and defocus weaknesses.

- *Economic*—Parents of disabled children will do everything in their power to make sure their child is accommodated. This "love" can become enabling and harmful. Through simple participation in sports, disabled youth and adults are provided the

44

opportunity and awareness of what it takes to succeed and to rebound. Hundreds of thousands of dollars are inversely affected with the participation of one person, depositing money into the tax base rather than debiting.

- *Spiritual*—Spiritual relationships are personal, useful and suggested. Sports present opportunities for the participant to immerse in ego. At some point in an athlete's career, egocentricity (losses) reveals humility. Compassion for others and an appreciation for limitations, opportunities and surroundings are exposed. It takes contrast to truly learn this lesson. Sports help a person develop a balance between ego and spirituality.

Wheelchair fencing requires the competitor to strap to a base and face his opponent, eliminating the "break away" used by an able-bodied fencer. I embrace the metaphor here of facing our fears and risking it all. Engaging life is facilitated through the *mechanism* of wheelchair sports. Competition taught me how to celebrate my victories and to get back up after my failures. I owe wheelchair sports.

Chapter Seven

Sometimes I am able to touch more lives through the acceptance of a loss than a win.
❋ *Paralympic gold medalist, Ricky Molier*

Failing Forward

One of the hardest losses for me was winning a bronze medal in Atlanta at the 1996 Paralympic Games. I had been in Paralympic Games in other countries before but never a combined and promoted competition on our own soil. Since 1980, the Paralympics was to be held in the same city as the *regular* games. Incidentally, to the disabled population, *regular* is a type of fuel used in motors. With the Olympics in Los Angeles, the entire disabled sports world looked forward to 1984 with great anticipation. But in a bold move, a few of the wheelchair sports leaders of the day attempted to invoke what they thought would be an improvement for wheelchair athletes by separating the disabilities. When it collapsed, the "wheelies" were defaulted to England to compete at Stoke Mandeville, the home of Sir Ludwig Gutmann and ironically the birthplace of wheelchair sports. The only way some disabled individuals get a chance to come to our country is through an international sports trip. This isn't ego talking here, athletes from other countries personally told me how disappointed they were. It was difficult to attend these games as an American. We were booed during the opening ceremonies.

When the Olympics was awarded to Atlanta, it inspired pride for American wheelchair athletes but struck a raw nerve in the international athletes who were lucky, or unlucky enough to have been around for the 1984 debacle. Wheelchair sports *pied piper* Andy Fleming was named Executive Director of the Atlanta Paralympic Organizing Committee, which gave the wheelchair athlete community confidence that America would rise to the task. Fortunately, the city poured out its heart and pocket book for the Paralympics and APOC was successful. Sunrise Medical deserves kudos as well for supporting the games with money and manpower.

My personal goals were historic because before Atlanta, no other athlete had competed in three different summer Paralympic games and won gold medals in three different sports. I had raced in 1984 at Stoke and played tennis in 1992 in Barcelona, winning gold in each sport. If I were to win a gold medal as a member of the U.S.A. Basketball Team, my "hat trick" would be complete. Gathering every couple of months for U.S.A. basketball camps, coaches Brad Hedrick and Lew Shaver had groomed us over a three-year period. We also trained individually every day for two to three hours above working full-time jobs.

Once I was in the gym in Georgetown at seven a.m., shooting free throws before going to work, and I had tears in my eyes because my mom had been diagnosed with cancer and was about to go through the big three (bone marrow transplant, radiation, and chemotherapy). A kid noticed my tears and said, "Hey, keep practicing, you'll get better."

Upon arrival in Atlanta, the residue of the Olympics was everywhere, from the performances of Carl Lewis, to the sacrifice of Keri Strug, the golden shoes of Michael Johnson, and the disturbing bombing in Centennial Park. The day of the opening ceremony finally came. Then two days later our first game matched us against Iraq, who never showed. Playing an inner squad game for the fans, we later discovered the Iraqis had sent CBS a fundraising packet requesting support for their team. Defeating Japan, Holland and Canada, we advanced to the medal round and faced Australia in the semifinal game.

> *Just because you are winning doesn't mean you are doing well.*
> ✳ *University of Texas men's basketball coach,*
> *Rick Barnes*

Lead by the renowned Troy Sachs, the Australians had nothing to lose and played fearlessly. The lead changed hands many times, but in front of 11,000 mostly American fans, we lost to the underdog Aussies 63–57. From an individual perspective, what hurt was I had done my homework. I was prepared. Coming off of the bench, I hit my first seven shots as the entire crowd was cheering, "Randy, Randy, Randy," but I didn't play down the stretch. It's difficult to accept when people don't believe in us like a coaching staff or my doctor just after my injury, but it's part of life. Steve, a gunshot victim from Utah and team member said, "Wow, you were ready. I guess all those years of pressure during other international competitions really prepared you." This statement confused me since I thought we were chosen for that reason. Not unlike coworkers or the family unit, basketball is a *team* sport and *we* lost that gold medal. It was disappointing for the *entire team*.

More heartfelt losses have been people I cared for. In the final at the Swiss Open in 1993, I had lost the first set and was losing the second to Laurent Giamartini of France. Playing at the Swiss Open required a quick study in French since the score was called in this language.

My best friend, Greg Gibbens, and I were at the Swiss and had been in Europe for two months. We were burned-out on Euroboys, Euroculture and the Euroattitude, badly craving anything American. Trust me, after two months in Europe, just hearing an operator say "Hi, this is ATT, may I help you?" has a very sweet ring. After spending time in a foreign country where they only speak their language, one can begin to understand entire conversations without even recognizing a word. Once I went to a very crowded club in Tel Aviv where everyone was eating and drinking, and dancing on the tables to "Hava Negelah." After several hours of the true Jewish party scene and the alcohol taking its toll, the wheelchair tennis players around me simply forgot I couldn't speak Hebrew. Points would be explained or jokes would be yelled in the crowd with enthusiasm and energy, and we would just laugh. I was laughing out loud and couldn't understand a word they were saying.

The sound of kids playing in a water-faucet behind center court was distracting me from my match. I kept asking for support with the problem, but the referee would not acknowledge my pleas; after all, I was an American. Before long I noticed that the distraction was removed, the water had stopped. At the next changeover I looked through the fence and saw 25 confused kids standing around the fountain. Greg was right next to the fountain involved in a "stand off" blocking them from the spout. They just stared at him as he kept shaking his head saying, "No more water."

Greg was an amazing man who had talent and a love of life like no other. He was Jean Lafitte reincarnate. He was painfully good looking, his personality was addicting, and everyone loved him. He was one of the most talented, unselfish and amazing people I have ever met.

They found Greg in his apartment on October 20, 1995. He had died of a gunshot wound to the head. Greg was my "Gus" in *Lonesome Dove*. He was gone. From his personal perspective of wheelchair confinement, Greg always said what he missed most was "walking in the woods."

> *No distance of space or length of time can reduce the value good friends have for one another.*
> ✳ *Robert Southey*

People we love occupy a spot in our center. They are woven into our being. When we lose someone or something, there is a huge hole that is never filled. At some point, the loss is *patched* with other people and experiences, but the *memory scar* exists forever. Life is an ongoing struggle with highs and lows. Success is the desired outcome but it's the struggles in our lives, competitive or personal, that teach us the most valuable lessons. At Central Texas Treatment Center, my counselor wouldn't let anyone get a Kleenex for someone crying. The box could be tossed to the floor with the person *in growth* getting their own Kleenex. Nothing was learned from a rescue.

Wheelchair sports have provided me valuable opportunities for growth. Certainly the opportunities to succeed are cherished, but over the years it has been *pushing forward* after the failures that has afforded me the greater lessons.

> *Life is full of peaks and valleys; we endure the valleys, and…Oh, do I love those peaks.*
> ✳ *Marilyn Hamilton*

Bits and Pieces

Bryna, one of the most positive people in the world, touched me deeply with this poem. Wherever you are…I thank you.

People important to you, unimportant to you, cross your life, touch it with love and carelessness and move on. There are people who leave you, and you breathe a sigh of relief and wonder why you ever came in contact with them. There are people who leave you, and you breathe a sigh of remorse and wonder why they had to go away and leave such a gaping hole. Children leave parents, friends leave friends, acquaintances move on, people change houses, people grow apart. Enemies hate and move on. Friends love and move on. You think of the many that have moved into your hazy memory.

You look at those present and wonder.

In God's masterful plan of lives, He moves people in and out of each other's lives, and each leaves a mark on the other. You find that you are made up of bits and pieces of all who ever touches your life, and you are more because of it, and you would be less if they had not touched you. Pray that you accept the bits and pieces of humility and wonder, and never question and never regret.

Chapter Eight

Precursor—From My Chair

In my opinion, the ignorance and frustrations that accompany a disability eventually took Greg's life. Comments made to him like, "I bet you were a hunk before you got hurt, weren't you," collected. *If there are no tools to deal with these frustrations*, they eventually can hit a saturation point.

I was in Boston teaching tennis and had trained with an able-bodied coach for two hours working on heavy balls and intense mobility. Notwithstanding the quality of training with wheelchair players, an able-bodied training partner sets a much higher pace, over-preparing you to handle the wheelchair game. I then conducted a wheelchair tennis camp for 35 players and finished with a presentation to coaches about the similarities and differences of our sport. Having already done more than 99.9% of the people in America, I arrived back at the hotel and prepared for the evening banquet.

As I was entering the elevator, a gentleman held the door for me. I still don't know why people do this. Elevator doors have crushed no one. During the ride, he made some demeaning eye contact, looked down at my legs and said, "You're just crippled, aren't you?" I fought off the urge to "snarl" and employed the tolerance and patience asked of society. Then he said, "You can't feel anything, can you? It must be horrible."

I understand his discomfort and ignorance yet where does it come from? I picture Elevator Guy as a kid, with his father years back, watching a television report about someone like wheelchair outdoorsman Mark Wellman, climbing a mountain and his father saying "Damn cripples, ought to be in a home." And then Elevator Guy absorbing his father's idea of the disabled and saying, "Yeah, ought to be in a home." Then he develops, breeds and passes it on to others.

After *pounding* tennis balls with John McEnroe and Steve Welch at an exhibition in Florida in front of a large crowd, I laid my racket on the ground so I could transfer into my everyday chair. A ball kid ran over, picked it up and handed it to me. I understand he was trying to be nice and I said thank you, but what's interesting is the shift in perception between the skill necessary to hit tennis balls with McEnroe, and a helpless person in a wheelchair not being able to reach the ground. My portrayal of a highly skilled athlete did not override the firmly established idea that a person in a wheelchair needs help.

We attempt to exist in between the two statements of "do you need any help?" and "you better slow down or you are going to get a speeding ticket." If we acquiesce, we are a doormat. If we challenge, we are angry. The middle is difficult to achieve. As John Hockenberry says, if either one of these comments is made, we have lost.

Without being in the *wheels* of someone who exists in a wheelchair, this is difficult to understand. My mom is a cancer survivor. She understands these sentiments and reluctantly goes to bank meetings with my step-dad. The comments of "Oh, you look so good," or "You are really doing well," offend her. She would frustratingly say, "I am doing just fine." Mike Watson is a great wheelchair tennis player who has just survived cancer as well. Upon greeting him at the U.S. Open Championships in San Diego, in an unintentional yet maudlin manner I said, "Hey Mike, how's it going?" He said, "Don't give me that crap." I said, "Is it that obvious?" "Yes it is." When I asked him about the similarities of sympathy, he said, "It's exactly the same."

In order to overcome this ignorance and these stereotypes we must *assertively* work together. The mission is clear, the challenge is grand, but it will take all of us making a stand. Just as one feather on a bird is ineffective, so is one person. But something as insignificant as a feather working together can empower movement of an entire "body." Together, we can soar!

Chapter Nine

> *I have just awoken in the Paralympic village after arriving in Sydney. The excitement in the cafeteria last night was total animation. So many different people from so many countries, coming together after experiencing so much. It reminds me of my 25-year high school reunion. I love it here!*

International Competition

Webster describes a patriot as "one who is proud of their country," but in my opinion it isn't that simple. There is a fine line between patriotism and egotism. When people and countries begin to force their will and ideas on others it becomes egotism, which clearly is insecurity.

Patriotism takes effort, education and maintenance. It's like a muscle, when it's flexed it becomes stronger, when it isn't, it atrophies. Its about borders, similarity and commonality, but it doesn't extinguish individuality or diversity. Just because you are born in a country, doesn't mean you're patriotic. I watched the Super Bowl in 1993 in Australia and was perturbed when no one listened during our National Anthem. With all due respect to the Aussies as they truly define patriotism, the incident tapped a patriotic root. Hey, that's my national anthem. Like love, it is a *developed relationship* that asks you to simultaneously sacrifice, endure and be patient. Don't parents love their children regardless?

The "American Dream" is having the *right* to dream and the *freedom* to turn those dreams into realities. Ever since I was a kid, I dreamed of competing for America, coming from behind and winning at the last second for flags, fans and pride. I grew up across from the high school in Pampa, Texas, and had the privilege of watching the great Olympic shot-putter, Randy Matson, train every day, throwing implements over and over. Wandering over from my home on Russell Street to the "Harvester" practice field, I would watch this mass of humanity train and listen to him talk about *the dream*.

After my injury, competing for the United States was the last thing on my mind. I was more concerned which one of my friends I

58

could ask to pull me up the stairs each morning at my high school. As time passed though, I became stronger and more functional, and eventually let the Trojan Horse in. My first wheelchair sports experience was actually conceived in 1979 at the University of Texas. It was Anna Hiss Gym where I cut my teeth. Jim Hayes from Arlington unselfishly drove the four-hour, one way trip, to conduct a clinic for "the boys" one night and after his prompting, I quickly developed my talent. My name began to circulate around the country and the option of competing for the U.S.A. became a reality.

In 1981, Bruce Karr, coach of the United States wheelchair basketball team, called to inform me that I had been nominated for a squad that would tour Japan for two weeks all expenses paid, and wanted to know if I could attend. I didn't think about that decision very long. Once I accepted, I became the first Texan to make a U.S. sports team. Can you imagine my excitement? Just 4 years earlier I was taking oil painting lessons, searching for something I could do from a wheelchair. This international sports *opportunity* opened the eyes of my family, friends and me, as to the possibilities. Other than to Mexico, which to Texans is really a district of the state, I had not traveled out of the country. The self-confidence I attained from being selected immediately converted me from an unsure "fresh cord" (new spinal cord injured person) to a confident athlete patriotically representing his country.

The irony of this tour was that I would be facing an entirely new culture from an entirely new culture. At four years post accident, I was still an apprentice of the "New World" in which I lived. There would be important learning externally and from within.

When a person makes the decision to attempt to go to the Paralympics, they put their life on hold. A key is turned in the ignition of an internal motor that is only turned off when the games are over. To an outsider, a Paralympian's life seems unbalanced yet to the athlete, the balance is more delicate than the immune system of a newborn. Every waking moment during a Paralympic campaign, an athlete must think about his game, asking, "Is it still there…do I still have it today?" Great athletes aren't just great; they are great when they need to be great. Certainly there is solace in just "knowing you're going," but it isn't over until the athlete loses or the flag goes up. And imagine the fitness level of a Paralympic athlete. In my racing days, my body fat hovered at 7%, my resting heart rate was just over 45 and my confidence was *packed*. I wasn't a wheelchair athlete,

I was an athlete that used a piece of athletic equipment. The familiarity we had with our bodies and sports chairs was similar to a blind man maneuvering in his home.

Winning a gold medal takes living a gold medal, it's a life-style, which must be present every conscious moment. Did you ever wonder why Michael Johnson wore gold shoes while he raced? Rest assured this act carried more value than the simple euphemism of winning gold. It fed his belief. In every decision made, every action taken, every bit of interaction with life, on and off the court, awake or asleep, a contender lives a gold medal. In a way, ownership of a gold medal is known before the athletes even arrive, simply due to their lived demeanor. With all due respect to Steve Welch, Australian David Hall had won the gold medal for tennis in Sydney months before.

A Paralympian's sacrifices must be definitive. I recall a popular advertisement during my 1984 Olympic run, which set two workers sweeping in the stands of a large stadium after a sporting event. As a young kid came out onto the track, one of the guys said, "Hey Joe, look, that kid's out there again." The young athlete put down some books, slipped on some oversized track shoes, set up in the starter's stance at the 400- meter mark and ran an all out sprint. Cramming oxygen back into his lungs, he again pulled up to the blocks. Mystified, the two older gentlemen paused while staring at the seemingly masochistic adolescent. This ad struck an emotional chord in me. It reminded me of the hours and hours my coach and I spent alone on that track in pursuit of our dream. This sacrifice though, is not unlike that of a single parent preparing lunches early in the morning for sleeping children on a school day or a business owner at his office late at night wondering from where his next client will come.

In my personal opinion, Paralympians are better athletes than our able-bodied counterparts. We work just as hard, do it for a lot less money, carry education to our venue as well as competition and overcame a major debilitating accident to arrive. Our stories display the true resiliency of mankind, therefore better matching us with the way life really exists. Though people have been sold the idea that Olympic athletes are *the perfect version of man*, in reality they are the athletes who *don't* represent society. We represent the idea that competitiveness is more than how hard you train. I hope it never happens, but could some of the top pro basketball players today truly accept and succeed in wheelchair basketball?

One of the most rewarding benefits of international competition is the exposure to people and their cultures. The Eastern Europeans have migrated all over Western Europe just as the Central Americans to the United States, and the Chinese to…well, everywhere.

After packing their own parachutes, Martin Legner and his friends would leap off the mountains and bridges of Austria and rob gravity as they would soar to the earth below. As life can change in an instant for any of us, a thermal pushed Martin back into the mountain from where he jumped, causing him to crash and break his back. He now runs his farm from his chair and is one of the best wheelchair tennis players in the world. I stayed with him once on his farm and met his wife, Doris, and his wonderful family.

Helping him on his farm was a family of six from Russia. The father tended to the animals, while the mother raised the children and ran the kitchen. She would ring the dinner bell and call every-one from the fields. I felt like I had a cameo in "The Sound of Music." I spent additional time with the family and learned that the farmhand was actually a nuclear physicist, but they had to leave their country because there just wasn't any work. Can you imagine having to pack up your family and relocate into Mexico or Canada? What would you prioritize when packing? Which direction would you go? What would you say to your children? Imagine the lan-guage barriers and the fears. He told me of 40% unemployment in his country, and that there was much corruption and compromis-ing. I was shocked to hear the things some of the Russians did to get money to buy food.

Once I was playing a Russian tennis player in Belgium and during the match I sensed some subsurface mockery towards him, that most of the Europeans were pulling for me. After the match I asked if my intuition was true and learned that Russians were cul-turally considered subordinate. Reinforcing the stereotype, this ob-servation took place at the same time a Russian submarine sank off the coast of Norway, killing all of its servicemen.

I know discrimination. I experience it everyday. What's inter-esting is that there is sub-discrimination within a discriminated group. This human habit *can* be eliminated with education and will.

Competing overseas challenged my perspective and enlight-ened me to a unique view of the world. Wars, accidents, plagues and birth defects have presented afflictions forever. Culturally and eth-nically, the way disabilities are treated hide or expose a country's empathy and fear and reveal its real personality. I have been shunned in restaurants, sped away from by taxi drivers, and skipped over by customers while in a line for food. Conversely, I have also been treated as an international ambassador. I was shocked to see young polio athletes in Barcelona, Atlanta and Sydney. Since this disease has been eradicated in the States, polio is disturbing to Americans. But to developing nations, polio is common. To some societies, disability means failure, weakness and undignified death. In other countries, like Holland or Australia, wheelchair athletes are accepted, respected and honored.

Living as a white able-bodied male in Texas and a disabled athlete has granted me two perspectives. Discrimination, selective judgment, or placing one above another because of ethnic, economic, gender, geographic, religious, cultural or physical differences is definitely wrong. We can't change overnight, but if one of us is God's child, then aren't we all? Don't all colors bleed into one?

Rewards

International competitions are ethnically magnificent. There is no predetermined mold of acceptability at the Paralympics. It's like bouillabaisse with all those wonderful yet diverse pieces seafood jumbled together in the common medium of sport. Watching a quadruple amputee swim, or a blind runner in the 1500-meters or a dwarf slam on some table tennis, carries valuable lessons about adapting, persevering *and utilizing what we have* in order to achieve. These lessons aren't just for common folk. With each of my Paralympic competitions I have been able to "see further."

An opening ceremony is the only day during the games that an athlete can genuinely enjoy. Each athlete "attempts" to put off the real reason they are there for a brief moment of gratitude. It is a humbling moment coming into a stadium of thousands of fans, surrounded by countrymen that have made similar sacrifices. Approaching the sound of 100,000 cheering people is like drifting in a canoe through a tunnel towards "obstructed view" white water; there exists a unique combination of anticipation and anxiety.

John Riggins was to be honored during the halftime of a football game at RFK Stadium in Washington, but he worried event organizers before the ceremony because he wasn't there. As the other honorees were about to be introduced, in full uniform Riggins came running out onto the field to the sound of 100,000 cheering fans. When asked by Joe Theisman why he did it, Riggins said, "Joe, I had to hear it one more time." Trust me, from the epicenter, thousands of screaming people gets in your blood.

And certainly participation is grand, but the anticipation for the Paralympics carries a staggering amount of energy as well.

> *Yes I love to eat honey…but there is that moment…*
> *just before I begin that is so much better.*
> ✳ *Winnie the Pooh*

Upon participation as a paralympian, a door is opened to a very secret place that will never be closed. Changed forever, you obtain a degree of knowledge that others, who have never made an international team, will never know. It's like hearing the very first cry of your first born or surviving a war. These events are perhaps meaningless to the ones who have not participated, but to the Paralympian, the change is understood.

If enough work has been done and greatness arrives, winning a gold medal opens a window to the soul, where every emotion ever felt, is kept. At the moment your opponent is defeated, there is a rush of uncertainties. As if eliminating the last of 12 warriors, after being cornered for ten days, psychologically the effort continues because it has been the only thing known for months. For just a moment you wonder, "is it really over?" Reality then permeates with congratulations coming from everywhere. With concurrent envy and respect, everyone within sight, including the warrior, who spent the last four years of his life preparing for your place, is looking right at you as your national anthem is played and your flag is raised. The moment however doesn't hold a candle to the value of the everlasting memory.

According to an ideological society, advertising tells us who we are *supposed* to be. Olympic ads can be very effective, capturing our hearts with powerful stories and messages. The distraction is the attachment of the corporate sponsor to the story, which sometimes can ruin the moment. If done in good taste though, advertisements can take us to the emotion of what these experiences are about.

Reminiscing after my silver medal victory, I rested in our dormitory at the University of Southern California campus after the men's 1500-meter exhibition race in Los Angeles in 1984. Immersed in ads, our television was continuously on. A favorite commercial of mine presented a plant manager in an office, in a manufacturing facility, watching a woman's gymnastics event on a small black and white television. As a little American athlete was called to perform, the manager grabbed a microphone and called for the employees to break, stating "She's on, she's on…get in here, let's go." The little gymnast appeared, then committed herself and competed with all her heart, as the crowd in the plant clapped in the background. As the camera panned their emotions, tears swelled in me. Some clapped, some cried, but all eyes were glued on that television and I was reminded of how many people are connected by someone's dream. But the burden of carrying the weight of a community and country on your shoulders is tremendous, especially when you find yourself losing.

In Barcelona, we had just won the semi-final match, earning the right to compete for the gold medal. We couldn't even leave the center due to the fact that so many fans wanted autographs. In frustration I was signing the autographs in haste, voicing our need to make the next bus. My tennis coach Dr. Moore said, "You sign every one of those, you will long for this moment some day." In Sydney, we would remove our credentials before traveling through Olympic Park because the delay of committing to signing autographs could be hours. The other day I informed some neighbors that I had just made the Paralympic team and was on my way to Sydney. It was the emotion on their luminous faces that truly captures what international sports are about. The excitement and honor that is brought to them from simply knowing you is a cherished responsibility, which I welcome. International competition is about countries and people and places and passion.

Proficiency at one thing becomes an aperture to many other opportunities. By becoming the best wheelchair tennis player in the world, gates have opened for me that definitely would not have been there otherwise. Advice I regularly provide for kids is whatever it is, become good at it. Develop it "fully and completely" and *expand your presence* with this skill. As Emerson says, "Develop your portion." Wheelchair sports have afforded me some wonderful experiences. The purpose here is not to boast but to emphasize the supplementary value of the *mechanism*.

I rode in a hot-air balloon over the Czech Republic border, sailed a 38-foot sail boat around the Cape of Good Hope in South Africa, and witnessed a pack of female lions take down a zebra at a wild game preserve. In the same body of water in which the infant Moses was placed, I swam in the Jordan River, and placed a hastily written prayer in a crease at the Wailing Wall in Jerusalem while listening to chanting Muslims worship the Koran in the distance. From the top of Masada, I have viewed the deteriorated Roman campsites that guarded the city 2,000 years ago, while overlooking the Dead Sea and the cave where the Scrolls were found.

I sat at the top of the ski jumps of the Innsbruck and Sapporo Winter Olympics, and in Munich I saw the dormitory where the Israeli athletes were held captive and the pool where Mark Spitz won his seven gold medals. I witnessed the graves of Darwin, Churchill and Freud at Westminster Abbey, received a torch from President Clinton that was lit from Martin Luther King's grave, shook Vice President Gore's hand (he was almost the President) and gave President Bush a hug.

From the top of Haliakela, at 10,000 feet, I have witnessed geese flying below me and scuba dived with sea turtles and humpback whales in Hawaii, and lay under the statue of Christ overlooking the Bay of Lisbon in Portugal. I have witnessed live brush fires in Australia's outback and flown 1,000 feet over the Opera House in Sydney Harbor. I was at a mass blessed by the Pope and have lain on the floor of the Sistine Chapel, admiring the works of Michelangelo. From museums in their home countries, I have enjoyed the paintings of Monet, Van Gogh, Rembrandt and Picasso.

After conducting a tennis camp in Japan for athletes from seven different Asian countries, "Happy Birthday" was sung to me simultaneously in six different languages at a surprise party, over real sushi (no California rolls there).

Since words don't do justice in describing my emotions, I have forgone the attempt. To the ones responsible for exposing me to wheelchair sports, I am truly grateful.

> *...and those are the memories that make me a*
> *wealthy soul.*
> ✳ *Bob Seger*

Chapter Ten

The Art of War

I was a successful athlete before my injury. I had won some important tennis matches and played well on my high school basketball team, but I was no where near the quality of athlete that I have become in a wheelchair. Somewhere along the way I tweaked my ability to perform well and to win and I am sure my success is directly related to surviving and overcoming my accident. The problem solving after an injury is very similar to fighting for your country; if it is *unconditionally desired*, it will be done.

During all my competitions, the training, the sacrifices, wins and losses, I learned a great deal about "periodization" or the timing of a peak performance. I developed the ability to win when it counted, believing that pressure was not a time for apprehension but an opportunity for greatness. As I have matured, I am more aware of the lack of fear I had back then, and it scares me. To quote a famous musician, "I wish I didn't know now what I didn't know then."

I will share some of these philosophies with you because I feel not only do they apply to athletic endeavors, but to life situations as well.

A Few Good Men

As the level of competitiveness increases, any weakness becomes more serious and eventually translates into death. In order to win, a person must be *honest* about what their weakness is, *open-minded* to attempt things that will eliminate the weakness, and *willing* to endure the pain of changing the deficiency. If an athlete wants to be great, that's *how* he does it. Only a few athletes will become great. Athletes can be grouped into three basic categories.

Are you a comfort competitor?

Most athletes are comfort trainers. Comfort training pacifies the athlete because the only work being done is comfortable. Comfort trainers go through the motions without any value or quality to a session. There is no challenge, only mediocrity. Comfort trainers will train, but only *when* it is convenient, it won't be difficult.

Are you an ego trainer?

An athlete that chooses ego training involves himself in training that is challenging but only in the areas he is *already proficient*. For example, a player who is skilled at cross-court forehands may decide to work for two hours on intense cross-court forehands, but this will be his favorite shot. He isn't working on his weaknesses. In sales, it would be like growing your existing accounts rather than finding new business. An ego trainer will train hard but only in an area that he likes.

Are you a growth trainer?

A true champion involves himself in growth or solution training. A growth trainer immediately goes to the weakest part of his game and *attacks it* for the purpose of eradicating the deficiency. There is an acute understanding that a weakness will be exposed during battle, which will make match-life finite. This athlete will spend time in the *specific areas* and the *most difficult situations* of an anticipated competition. For a long distance racer, there is a huge difference between the decision-making during social miles and the fringe of anaerobic threshold. I can't emphasize how important this point is. These sessions won't be much fun but there is always *pain* to pay, which can be *pained* now or *pained* later. Growth trainers love *pain*.

As with able-bodied sports, most wheelchair athletes are recreational and some are semi-competitive. There are only a few true champions. To achieve greatness, a true champion will continuously break down his game, with brutal honesty, to give himself the best chance of winning.

PIG

I remember once in kindergarten attempting to trace a pig that was under a sheet of paper on my desk. Even though my pig didn't match the perfection of the model, the detail of the image provided a guideline for what I was attempting to do, thusly resulting in a fair match. One of the most significant guidelines I have used in sport enlists the principles of Preparation, Improvement and Goals, or the guideline of the PIG.

Preparation determines the difference between the reality perspective of "yeah baby" versus "oh no." At some point during a competition, an athlete recognizes either sufficient or "yeah baby" *preparation*, or insufficient or "oh no" *preparation*. I would actually film my opponents through the windscreens behind the courts to eliminate individual graphics and reveal specific body language, giving me a clue as to where their shots were being hit. While my opponents were socializing, I spent many evenings reviewing tapes and studying body position. An athlete must train with the footsteps of his opponents in his ears. I loved getting into a U.S. Open final and during the second or third game, knowing I was better *prepared* and under my breath saying, "yeah baby!"

Next, focusing on perfection is unresalistic because it magnifies the pressure of reaching the goal. With the understanding that an athlete will make mistakes, focusing on *improvement* reduces this pressure. *Improvement* avoids the labeling of good or bad, as he focuses on adjustments over judgments. These simple adjustments create *present focus*, which prevents the athlete from being distracted from the desired result. In our pre-game pep talk at the regional basketball tournament in Birmingham, we were about to play Mobile who had beaten us the three previous meetings. I reminded the team that mistakes were a part of sport and were going to happen, and I encouraged the team to let them go. If we focused on our *improvement* throughout the game, our desired outcome of going to the Final Four would appear less significant and carry less pressure. We won the game in overtime and went on to the "Big Dance" in Chicago. Progress, not perfection.

The G is for *goals*, which sets up a road map *towards* success. Even if the *goal* is simple, a human being is more likely to succeed if he knows where he is going. In my opinion, an athlete too often sets an indelible plan and stubbornly sticks to *goals* set using old data. When these *goals* aren't met, judgment can tell him he is failing. With continuous change in life, he shouldn't be afraid of "adjusting" his plan. Even if his *goals* don't set benchmark workout standards, some type of *goal* is encouraged.

Over the years, when I focused on these items rather than the reciprocal, more times than not, I maximized my performances.

> *Every man can fight…but the real test of a man is if he can think.*
> ✳ *Braveheart*

Practice Winning Everyday

Here's my spin about being healthy, training and winning.

International athlete and coach Bruce Karr said, "If you're involved with a friend in competition, treat the friendship like a robe. Take it off during the event then put it back on after the match." I agree.

I strongly believe in distributive practice over mass sessions. Lengthy training programs can cause an athlete to lose focus. For a one-week period a person will develop more from three, one-hour sessions than one, three-hour session. I call this "visiting" the sport; it should be done often, just like "visiting" your family. The Mexican Racing Machine, Saul Mendoza, told me that the morning before he raced in the Olympics in Sydney, he went to the practice track, hopped into his racing chair and completed ten very easy laps. He then returned to his dormitory, showered and went back to sleep. Even though he didn't physically challenge himself that morning, the "visit" served as a reminder of his commitment to the sport which he used the remainder of the day, until the event that night. Saul Mendoza won the gold medal.

I also believe in quality sessions over quantity. Dr. Bal Moore taught me about the importance of training specificity. I was in discussion with an Australian once about how difficult the upcoming Paralympics would be for him because of the pressure of competing in front of fellow countrymen. He "morseled" that in order to get ready, they had done some practice competitions in front of some very large crowds. I said, "Oh really, some big crowds?" He wasn't getting the point. Practice for the Paralympics isn't really practice because it's…practice. True environments cannot be duplicated. The point here is to be mentally aware, especially during a paralympic competition, that it will be larger than planned. In a team sport like basketball or tennis doubles, that's why proven athletes are selected in the crunch. Larry Bird said, "There are hundreds of great players in the NBA, but the number of players that can hit the shot when it really counts can be counted on one hand." Can you say Reggie Miller?

In his book, *It's Not About The Bike*, Lance Armstrong said an athlete must suffer during training sessions because they will definitely suffer in a race. As I mentioned in growth training, the decision-making process is different for people in comfortable situations compared to duress. I believe athletes must spend time at the specific level of duress that most of the *decision-making* will take place. If the difference between aerobic and anaerobic training isn't fathomed, then quality training hasn't occurred. It isn't any more important than this; understand the psychology within the physiology of anaerobic training. *There is nothing more important than specificity of training.*

There exist three periods in which an athlete can train. He can prepare *before* the event and most likely perform well. In a panic situation, he can train *during* the event with a significantly lower chance of performing well. Or he can train *after* the event, which carries a great deal of remorse. Athletes, businesses or families who succeed, obviously spent time preparing.

The morning offers a "fresh mind," a clean sheet of paper that is clear of the many thoughts and images that are picked up throughout the day. Train (physically or mentally) in the morning for the best recall.

I spoke earlier of the brutal honesty necessary in weakness reduction. I also believe an athlete must have a weapon, must know what that weapon is and be able to *close* with that weapon. A great athlete pulls his competition to a chosen battleground where his tactic will be used to *close*. Whether stubborn consistency or a knifing underspin backhand, what will he use to *close*?

> *I've never lost a match. But I have run out of time before I figured out a way to win.*
> ✳ *Jimmy Connors*

A champion achieves more from the lack of making big mistakes than astonishing plays. I have found that it was the reduction of fear that contributed more to my success than the development of talent. Certainly we must develop our skills, but in the end it's the voice of doubt that destroys. We all have two basic internal personalities, a critic and a champion. Ignoring the critic and listening to the champion is essential. What a relief it was when Neanderthal Man discovered he could "make fire." What a relief it is when we realize the power we have in affecting our own attitude.

Healthy food doesn't taste good. Give me peanut better and jelly sandwiches and "cheeseburgers in paradise" all day long. I love food and eat like a Labrador Retriever. But real hunger sets in during mini fasts of three-quarters of a day, which *with seasoning* can make broccoli and cauliflower very tasty. I believe athletes should pay attention to the psychological contribution of food rather than the nutritional factor. The great Bill Tilden lived on steak and ice cream. Eat what makes you *feel* like a champion?

An athlete must avoid regrets, which will be carried forever. Make the best effort possible in whatever is attempted. Leave it on the court. Play every match like it will be over someday.

Positive affirmations posted in visible areas in one's environment act as indelible stamps of inspiration on our minds. If it is written down, later it is easier to recall. I would always put up P.A.'s in my hotel room or dormitory that would affirm my commitment. I carried around a photo of the U.S. Hockey Team with their hands held up in the air, just at the moment they beat Russia at Lake Placid in 1980. The effect on my emotion from looking at the photo was like pouring gas on a fire. An athlete knows he is in the right "emotional neighborhood" if, while visualizing the happiness of winning a gold medal during a training session, he has ever started to cry. This is a good sign. These were my positive affirmations written on a wall in my apartment in Barcelona.

> *I am fit*
> *I am a great tennis player*
> *I will always do my best*
> *I will push for every ball*
> *I will not judge…only adjust*
> *I will have fun*
> *I am alive*
> *Cool and intent, I will strike the ball*
> *It is my court, I am Randy Snow, the fighter*
> *I am the gold medalist at the 1992 Paralympics*
> *in Barcelona*

From *The Inner Game of Tennis*, W. Timothy Gallwey reminds us that the mind doesn't know the difference between image and reality. In order to reduce the anxiety of arriving on center court for my U.S. Open championships, through imagery I would mentally take myself to *the floor of the pit*. Just before the final, I would find a quiet place, and imagine being called by the referee, put my notes away, take my headphones off. I would transfer off the couch, push down the pathway and nod to my supporters and glance at those who envied me. I would guide my chair down the ramp breathing in Southern California, onto center court, make eye contact with my coach, strap into my Quickie chair, reach into my racket bag and pull out one of my "Excaliburs." I would feel the air, measure the electricity and literally smell the tennis balls. I would make this image as close to reality as possible. When the referee finally called me, I was much more comfortable having already dealt with the "butterflies." I had already *been there.*

A dance-club performed at a banquet once and impressed me with their intricacies and impeccable timing. I had the opportunity of spending time with one of the dancers after the show and asked, "How many hours do you practice?" I bonded with her when she asked, "Do you mean on the dance floor or in my mind?"

The mind has difficulty doing two things at once. If mistakes are being made, the key is to distract the mind from the mistake. If the desired task evades, relieve pressure by focusing on a past success rather than a failure. Eastern philosophy teaches the way to relieve pain is to focus on the same part of the body, on the other side. If an appropriate thought is unavailable, concentrate on a childhood room or a leaf on the court, a pet or the shoe strings on the shoes of a ball boy. I would take Monet postcards to the court in my racket bag and pull them out during the changeover. During a presentation in Cincinnati, I heard Steve Welch say he once focused on a spot on his opponent's shirt that he noticed during changeovers. Tricking the mind into nothingness is one of the most lucrative skills in being a champion.

I was shooting an ad for Quickie once in Longmont, CO and hadn't trained in two days; I really needed a "visit." It was eleven p.m. and the courts at the hotel were closed; yet after prowling around the fence, I found an open gate. Hoping to turn on the lights, I planned on hitting against a wall but the lights were locked off. I still went onto the unlit court and began doing some lateral mobility drills. Without visual stimuli, the more I pushed and shadowed shots, the more I found my visualization to be effective. I was able to clearly *see* my shots, pathways, and necessary outcomes, as this technique was lively. It was a subtle awareness reinforcing the benefit of visualization.

The taper or rest period is one of the most effective training tools available to an athlete. By taking time off just before an event, the body creates a natural craving for what it has spent an incredible amount of time doing. Rather than dulling the sharpness, the taper actually recharges the natural batteries and heightens the intellectual and emotional domains, which will improve performance. But I have a three-day rule. Just as days wear on a sandcastle, I never went longer than three days before I "visited" the "sandcastle" for maintenance. In sports and in life, know *the value of waiting*.

Confidence must be personalized. Deep down an athlete *must know* he is better than his opponent is and find the personal path to what works for him. When asked before the NBA Finals if he was a better player than Michael Jordan, Phoenix Sun Charles Barkley said, "If I think he is a better player than me, I have already lost." Even though he knew the correct answer, he also was aware of the psychology of success. Mark Spitz was not arrogant when he said he would win 7 gold medals, he was confident. Rather than fearing and avoiding a competitor, immerse in them, study them, find out that they are human and have weaknesses as well. This will boost your confidence. During the Olympic racing campaign in 1984, I placed pictures of Jim Knaub everywhere. This gave me a constant visual of my main competitor and rather than fear him, his awe lost its luster. The athlete who will win is the athlete who *makes the decision* to win.

At the top level of any competition, everyone is fit. Don't count on fitness or extra training as an advantage. The advantage will come from mental preparation. I am appalled at the minimal amount of mental toughness training taught at the Paralympic level to United States wheelchair sports teams. If you want to perform *under pressure*, have "practiced techniques" in place, know what they are. In my opinion, the best weapon at this level is reading. I always ask athletes, "What are you reading to improve your game?"

Balance in training is paramount. Athletes must be balanced on the court but it is the balance off the court that is preeminent. If distractions are renting space in an athlete's head, it will be more difficult to recognize "the zone." Destiny does not bring greatness often. When she comes, she may be refracted or disguised. Total balance in health, family, financial, and spiritual domains will provide a most prepared and aware athlete. Gold medals *are the athlete* and have to be lived, not just earned.

> *The athletes aren't necessarily better today, but there are definitely more of them.*
> ✳ *Texas women's basketball coach Jody Conradt*

Many have compared the great ones of the past to present-day athletes...could Rod Laver beat Pete Sampras, could David Kiley beat Pat Anderson, could George Murray beat Heinz Frei? Obviously there is no way of really knowing the answer. In defense of the great ones of the past, they used a *process* that allowed them to defeat all the athletes of their day. Bringing someone forward into a modern era, what leads one to believe that his process and work ethic wouldn't again push him to the top? If eras are to be compared, it isn't fair to compare how fast or how hard the ball is being hit, because the champions of the past didn't have the luxury of training against the same pool of athletes. To truly compare a lineage of champions in a specific sport, what must be compared is work ethic. *Who worked harder* is the only way to put past and present athletes on the same page.

Lastly, if the work has been done, the time on the court invested and the mental preparation correct, the first victory of an event isn't on the court, it's when the competitor's eyes meet for the first time. Early in my career, I remember warming up for a basketball game against David Kiley's team. I was making my best *effort* to put on my game face. Although we were friends, I had adopted the ferocity of a competitor, yet inside I knew it was false. As we simultaneously met each other during the pre-game lay ups, he looked at me and said, "Hey, you better get that frown off your face or I am going to get one." I imploded. The first battle of the war of a tournament is decided with the first contact. Don't look <u>at</u> their eyes, look <u>through</u> them.

The top 25 tennis players in the world have two things in common; none of them got there the same way and none of them quit. Nothing takes the place of persistence.
✳ *Randy Snow*

Chapter Eleven

> *Far better to dare a mighty thing, to win glorious triumphs, even though checkered with failure, than to rank with those poor spirits who neither enjoy much nor suffer much, because they live in the gray twilight that knows neither victory nor defeat.*
> ☀ *Theodore Roosevelt*

The Real Race

L essons from competition and their life applications are transparent. The expression *play the ball not the player* is often used in tennis. In life, the matching quote is *play the moment*, as we should concentrate on what's right in front of us. Placing expectations on our plans puts a great deal of pressure on us to *control* our lives, possibly setting us up for failure and misery. Competition teaches us how to sort out our problems under pressure, where we shift our process to fit into the overall goal. Using all our available resources, we build upon our strengths, focus on the problem at hand and *push forward* according to an ever-changing plan.

According to Dr. Bryce Young of the Van der Meer Tennis Academy, there are three basic stages of personal development attained during sport.

- The first stage is where we develop our *image,* we are proud of our bodies and our package, and we ripen our self-esteem. All-important *self worth* is developed here.

- The second stage is based in accomplishments, titles, on *personal achievements*. Examples of these *earnings* may be a college degree, landing of a big account or winning a gold medal.

- The final stage is the *statesman* stage. Here we find more compassion as we focus on *contributions* to our fellow man rather than what has happened on the outside. Examples are raising children, teaching a catechism class or conducting a wheelchair tennis camp.

Some never leave the *image* stage while others arrive at *statesman* early. In matters of maturity, the *statesman* stage will provide a more meaningful return. I have experienced more value in giving my tennis secrets to future champions than having them in my possession. It was with mixed emotion that my tennis career ended in Sydney, against the great Australian David Hall. With the full intention of ending his gold medal run, I held a certain level of pride knowing that eleven years earlier, I actually had him as a student in a tennis camp. *Personal achievements* invite us to say, "Wow, I did that." *Statesman* achievements afford us the opportunity to say, "Wow, I am glad I did that."

Dr. Young also helped me with the following *eureka*. As I was training for Sydney, my inner child cried out for another gold medal. But I had to ask myself, "Is that really what I want?" In a discussion about *why we continue to do sport*, Dr. Young said, "At this stage, it isn't about the tennis anymore. We play because there is no better place to learn about ourselves…about patience, focus and humility…it takes a great deal of emotional intelligence to deal with disagreeable things."

An old timer named Frank once told me to approach life like a cork floating down a river. Moving with the momentum of the water, a cork casually flows and adjusts to the current, going where the river takes it. Attempting to "control its situation", sometimes the cork reaches out and attaches itself to a limb. Thinking that it's in charge, it now bobs, tosses, goes under, panics and struggles with its existence. Eventually breaking away from the "attempt at control", in relief, it rejoins the flow of the river and enjoys *pushing forward*. If we can go into our journey like a cork floating down a river, rather than trying to be in control, certainly our experience will be much more pleasurable.

There will be many *tournaments* in life. First day at kindergarten, a school play, making the high school basketball team, a college report, proposing marriage, first child, selling a business, burying a loved one, writing a will, going to God…life is a cycle. To learn from these tournaments and not base our being on our performance is the key. Sport teaches us to flow.

> *Seek no legacy and you shall have one.*
> ✳ *Robert E. Lee*

Rear View Mirror

With the following words, I am disclosing myself for possible scrutiny, but if it helps one other person, then being candid here is worthwhile and much more useful than worrying about what other people think.

I have had many great opponents along the way. In racing, there was Jim Knaub, George Murray and Jim Martinson. Tennis presented Brad Parks, Laurent Giamartini and Steve Welch. Once in the final at the Ericcson Championships (The Lipton) at Key Biscayne, I overcame eleven match points to defeat Giamartini. And David Kiley was the greatest basketball player of all time. At one time or another, I beat them all. And if defeating these champions didn't establish my competitive prowess, then certainly absorbing a spinal cord injury reflects my mastery of worthy foes. But one opponent had always had my number. Cunning, baffling and powerful, that opponent had been drugs and alcohol.

If I could have changed one thing in my life, it wouldn't have been my accident or to have saved more money, it would have been that I sequestered this *opponent* early, when I first became aware of it. I never partied normally. I thought losing control was fun. It wasn't all the time and never during my competitions, but after big sporting events, it became a pattern of trouble.

One night after drinking, I dropped off some friends, then headed home, but forgot that my wheelchair was in the trunk of my car. After I sat honking in the driveway at three a.m., my sister, who was my roommate at the time, finally awoke. After unappreciatively transferring into my chair, I "slothed" into the kitchen. Staring into the stimulating offerings of the inside of my blurred refrigerator, I proceeded to consume several packets of beef jerky, and chased the chow with red Koolaid. I vaguely remember neither having much culinary value. As I lay in bed the next morning, my sister opened my door and asked what I had done with Buddy's dog jerky and the hummingbird food. As you may imagine, the aftertaste disgusted me. This was one of the funnier situations; there were much worse.

With any addictive and compulsive behavior, if one thinks there is a problem, there probably is. But there isn't a reason to change unless there are real consequences. Some call us recovering alcoholics, others chemically dependent. There are descriptions ad infinitum. The designation doesn't really matter, as the importance isn't in the title but the *acceptance of the membership*.

At first I was embarrassed. How could I deal with the accompanying pressure of international sports, yet be so weak? Just as many able-bodied people naively suggest how to overcome paralysis, it was brought to my attention that willpower was my problem. Attending track practice every day for eleven months and pushing a hundred miles a week, rain or shine, is willpower. I had willpower! Lord knows I tried as hard as I could, but this fight had a different set of rules. This problem definitely had to do with giving in rather than hanging on. It was like living in a wheelchair. The longer I denied it, the longer I would struggle.

A percentage of the disabled population migrates towards this form of escape. A pitying and enabling society awards passage without much repercussion. "They understand." But escape using drugs and alcohol kills people and it was going to kill me.

> *I have been driven to my knees many times because there was no place else to go.*
> ✳ *Abraham Lincoln*

After I had *made the choice* to allow my life to cave in, I was very fortunate when family and friends *persuaded* me into admitting my problem and I submitted to an intervention. Reluctant to admit, I was defeated, and committed to a long-term rehabilitation program for chemical dependency.

One afternoon, I was in a concrete recreational area that was isolated among several buildings. It was nothing more than a large dead room. In the context of comparison—try the track at the Los Angeles Olympics and a recreational area in a treatment facility for drugs and alcohol. After doing some cardiovascular exercise involving "short" interval sprinting, which I'm sure confused the staff, I was resting on the ground with my head drooping as I felt the endorphins. I was involved in severe mental bludgeoning about what I had done to myself, my family and the ones who loved me. I had everything and had lost it all. As I contemplated, I noticed that the sun had slipped high enough above the wall that its rays were hitting just above me. For one who had won ten U.S. Open Wheelchair Tennis Championships, I just couldn't believe I had *made choices* in my life that robbed me of my access to one of the greatest free gifts of life: the sun.

I transferred up into my chair and reached up to see if I could place my hand in its light. I could just barely reach it. How can I properly describe this moment? The fresh effect of feeling the sun powerfully struck an opening to someplace very nice and at that instant, a source of awareness told me that what I had used to validate my life was incorrect. As Ken Blanchard, author of *Leadership by the Book* describes, the problem is in our focus on "earthly desires." My boat, my 401K, my ranch house, people pleasing, worrying, where I was supposed to be, it all dominated me. That stuff *was* my existence.

In a few minutes, the sun dropped down to my face and I was energetically reminded of my potential. Just then a ladybug, making its way through the fence three stories down, landed on my arm. Wrapped in sun, she and I were the only living beings in the room. As tears rolled down my face I was overwhelmed with joy, even in that desperate place. I knew I was going to *push forward*.

> *Everything we do is a choice and one way or another, we will be accountable.*
> ✳ *Karen Korb, Paralympic tennis champion*

Before I allowed it to happen, I had a lot of money in the bank, a big boat in the drive, electronics galore and a "ranch home" on an acre of property. As my favorite thinker Jimmy Buffett said, "I had enough money to buy Miami…it was never meant to last," as I was miserable. When I was finally discharged from Central Texas Treatment Center, I had $15 and a suitcase with enough clothes to last for seven days. Gone were all my possessions and the stuff I thought was important. What I had left were my uncommonly valuable items. These were the important ones, the sentimental gifts, the pictures of people and places during my international trips, the items that I had saved over the years and the memories. More importantly what I had left was finally me.

For the first time in my life, I didn't have a trophy or a nice car or a trip or a picture with a President to validate myself. Living in a recovery house with seven other guys, I took the bus each day to my job where I sold Shriner's Circus tickets for a telemarketing firm. Enjoyable bus transport requires two criteria; get there early and bring a book. And each day I added a bit more security, friendship and self-esteem, and my life was pieced back together. I don't need to tell you that *starting over* is difficult, but sometimes, *it must be done*.

Am I endorsing these experiences as a necessary path to a leadership role? Many others have taken a path of less resistance. As I mentioned earlier, I am humiliated by this experience. But for me, I suppose it was necessary. No consequences, no reason to change! My hope for others is that this type of discovery is much simpler. If or when the wrong things become the validation in our lives, we endanger the well-being of our soul.

The secrets to healthy recovery mirror living with a physical disability. Awareness of the problem and re-establishment of worth are primary. Asking for help among the ones who have been there is important. And a spiritual side, a relationship with God is suggested. It is said, religion is for those who don't want to go to hell, but spirituality is for the ones who have been there. Spirituality is mortar. I look forward to living the rest of my life "one day at a time." Who knows what will happen in the future, but for me, I had to hurt enough to want to change. I finally experienced consequences strong enough that I decided to do something about it, which was to give up. It's done daily. Acceptance is the key, the first step towards being accountable, but we must be honest.

I have a huge "forgetter" which feeds the *rear view mirror complex*. Once the *opponent* was behind me, I thought it was less significant than it appeared. That is why the message in the mirror is:, "Objects in mirror are LARGER than they appear."

Looking back in front of me, today I do things differently with humility close by. As far as *pushing forward*, what other choice do we have? Entrepreneur and red fish guru Dub Gibbens brought tears to my eyes when he once said, "Son, I have lost a lot of money in my life and I tell you, I have always had more fun making it than having it." Thank you Dub, as we travel onward through the "Garden Canal of Life," in search of "big reds."

> *Of course I believe in miracles...I am one.*
> ❋ *John Lucas, NBA All-Star*

SECTION TWO

STORIES OF TRIUMPH

> *Some of it's magic, some of it's tragic,*
> *but it's a good life all the way.*
> ✳ *Jimmy Buffet*

Through my travels I have come across some very inspirational people. I believe God speaks to us through the wisdom we find in others. Though filled with what society labels as adversity, the following stories reveal the awareness of a deeper message about people, places and situations. These inspiring vignettes represent success and failure, with laughter and introspection. We must keep our eyes open to stories revealing personal wisdom and summon their power to accomplish and endure!

Chapter Twelve

One World

Perfect is not the way we want it, it's the way it is.
※ *Helon Thompson*

The Champp

I believe in angels. Unrecognizable by sight, they can only be detected by their actions. I went to Battle Creek, Michigan, to do a speech for Kellogg's once where I think I met an angel.

Doug was so big he had trouble leaning over to push my tennis chair to the limousine. I offered to help him but he giggled and said, "It's OK, I've got it." After loading my bags we left for "The Cereal City." To pass the time, my plan was to review my presentation. I really wasn't in the mood for talking, but Doug persisted. As we continued on the one hour drive, I offered the usual background stuff, informing him of my sports history and that I would be traveling to Sydney on the following Monday. He said, "I knew it, I knew picking you up was going to be great. When I saw on the paperwork that you were disabled I thought, all right, a guy in a wheelchair, I'm going to learn something from this guy. I feed off this kind of person." This was one of the most interesting comments I had heard and rather than repelled, I was drawn closer to him. As we continued, I became aware of his insight to high level athletics. I whined a bit about being 41 years old and having to compete against the younger athletes and he said, "Just be ready to die." This profound statement really got my attention and I said, "How do you know this?" Here is his story.

Doug grew up in Michigan playing football but his real love was boxing. In 1979 he was one of the best "light heavyweight" boxers in the United States and barely missed the U.S.A. boxing team that was going to Moscow. But as life is as unpredictable as an angry mother bear, the entire United States boxing team was killed in a plane crash on their way to Poland to prepare for the Olympics. Devastated, the U.S.O.C. was charged with the responsibility of filling another team and Doug was called. With mixed emotions, the "replacement" U.S. Boxing team again traveled to Poland and as they deplaned, the airport was filled with cheering and weeping supporters. For 10 days these athletes prepared for the 1980 Olympics against the Poles, Koreans, Russians, and Israelis, then flew to Moscow.

The gym in Petersburg was full of athletes when the Americans learned that Jimmy Carter had "pulled the plug" and America would boycott the Olympics. As word spread, the entire gym was heartsick, and especially the Russians who thought "What would a gold medal be without beating an American?" Doug came home, accepted the disappointment and began training for the 1984 Games in Los Angeles.

Over the next few years Doug refined his skill and in 1983 actually defeated Evander Holyfield to win the Goodwill Games. But just before the trials for Los Angeles, his physical fitness atrophied severely. For no apparent reason, he couldn't maintain any level of muscular or cardiovascular fitness. After completing check-ups with several doctors, he received the devastating news that he had cancer, and that it had filled his abdomen. In an attempt to save his life, he had emergency surgery that removed most of his colon, which placed him on an artificial system for the removal of his bodily excretions. He was told to "be ready to die." But designer drugs, a healthy diet, luck and a "wounded animal" attitude has kept Doug alive to this day. His boxing career and chances of being an Olympic champion are over. He now drives a limousine and is frequently asked to council terminally ill patients at the local hospital. Now it was my turn; I wanted something from him.

I asked him, "What do you say to your patients, where do you start, how do you know where to steer them?" These and many other questions were answered when he went through the acceptance process of death. He said he was reminded there was nothing we could do about death, that we all owed one. All of us would die someday. The question was, what frame of mind did we want to be in when we died? He would ask his patients, "Do you want to die happy or do you want to die sad?" The answer was always the same. Once there, he would compassionately encourage them to surround themselves with the things that made them happy.

I felt like I was in an Olympic time warp as I felt I had just heard one of the greatest stories ever. He informed me that he desired to remain anonymous but I said, "People need your message Doug," so he agreed to let me print. When I departed, I begged that he drive me to the airport. I was disappointed when it was another driver.

I know Doug exists or I think he does but I don't think I will ever see him again. I am reminded that time here is limited, that we are to live each day surrounded by the things that *make us happy*. Doug, wherever you are, Holyfield has nothing on you, man, nothing!

Who Is Packing Your Parachute?

There is psychology in the friends we choose. Some choose people that are worse off or not as smart so they feel strong. Others choose friends that challenge them to grow. I have been very fortunate to have been supported by an unconditional group of people that believed in me and challenged me throughout my career as an athlete and as a person. Surrounding ourselves with people that support us is as important as a cushion to a paraplegic.

An able-bodied athlete from Great Britain, Derek had made the 400-meter final in Seoul. His dream of winning a gold medal was shattered when, on the first turn, he tore his hamstring and fell to the track. After rehabilitating the hamstring, his gold medal dream continued as he began training for the Olympic Games in Barcelona. His father worked his regular job and at night managed a warehouse to help pay for his son's training.

Four years later the British trials were held and Derek not only made the team, but he again advanced to the final of the 400-meter event. He was the favorite to win the gold medal. The commentators were primed. One of them said, "And here is Derek Redmond, ladies and gentlemen, the favorite to win the gold, we will be telling his story for years to come." The announcer was correct, but not in the way he anticipated.

Derek had a great start but when he came around the first turn, the entire Olympic stadium and the rest of the world was devastated, as he fell to the track. Derek had torn the same hamstring. The other runners finished in world record times, then congratulated each other as they sought out the flags of their respective countries.

In a mix of agony and determination, to everyone's surprise Derek got up on his good leg and began hopping down the track. All eyes were on him as he struggled to *finish what he had started*. The cameras were focused on him until a scuffle in the stands drew their attention. Coming down the steps, pushing people out of the way was a big black man and on his shirt it said, "I am Derek Redmond's father." Despite the futile attempts of the officials, Mr. Redmond reached his son, who was now hopping in pain along the home stretch. When Derek saw that it was his dad, he burst into tears and collapsed as they crossed the finish line together.

Amending the poem "Footprints," in Derek's life that day there were *5 footprints on the track*. With the title of his book, a famous parachutist offered the question we all must consider, *Who Is Packing Your Parachute?*

> *When selecting flowers for a bouquet, always*
> *choose the best you can find.*
> ✳ *Rose Snow*

Gratitude

McDonalds had set up free stores in the athlete villages in Barcelona and in Sydney. Unfortunately, we had to avoid this food because it didn't have much nutrition. But as soon as I completed my games, I acquired a slight eating disorder called *reverse bulimia* and devoured Big Macs for the remaining few days.

As I previously queried, why must we lose something before we realize it is important to us? Losing the use of my legs *stands* out as my most poignant example of this human tendency. Appreciation of the moment will guarantee gratitude.

Finding access to laundry services is vital when traveling for long periods away from home. We were lucky in Atlanta because we could use the same facilities afforded the *real* athletes. By the way, to a disabled person, *reel* describes what a fisherman uses to catch fish. In Sydney the laundry service was free.

Once in the laundromat mat in Atlanta, I had two loads of clothes in machines and was watching them closely. U.S.A. clothing will be stolen for two reasons; athletes from third-world nations need clothes, and U.S.A. is written all over them. As I was reading my book, *The Seat of the Soul*, by Gary Zukov, I noticed an African athlete with polio loitering near a machine. I thought to myself "Aha," a thief, and I quickly became a spy and surreptitiously read and watched.

Not interested in his surroundings, the athlete would slowly open the door to this machine then gradually put the door down again. As I watched, he repeated the process… opening the door slowly until the machine stopped…then closing it again. Initially, I was confused, but it finally became clear. He was trying to figure out what was making the machine stop. He had probably come from a shantytown on the outskirts of a major city in the Congo or Zaire and obviously had never used a washing machine.

Emotionally involved in thought, I was caught by the African as he glanced my way, but the lesson I was learning had effected indifference. Instead of taking for granted my country's abundance in everything, my level of appreciation was boosted. But I also became aware of a deeper message. Whether a washing machine or God working in our life, it's not whether we know *how* He works, but that He *does* work that is important.

Another time we were in the lounge of our dormitory in Atlanta preparing for Japan. Not too tall but very fast, the Japanese were a threat to our gold medal and warranted detailed attention. Every night we reviewed statistics and videotape. Coach Brad Hedrick and I are of the same ideology in that specific preparation of an opponent is fundamental. But it was around eleven p.m. and I was becoming extremely bored with their minutiae. Plus I had not "star struck" the staff and knew my chances of playing time was not good. Double standard management will invite mutiny.

I had transferred off the couch to get some water when, knowing the Swedes were in the building next to us, I glanced outside the window. Involved in voyeurism, I picked up the silhouette of a wheelchair athlete leaning out of his chair into the "trash dumpster" down below. I noticed he was removing tires from the trash bin that the American racers and basketball players had discarded. No one wants to lose a Paralympic medal due to equipment distractions so in the United States, half-worn tires are replaced with new ones. In a brief moment of fresh gratitude, I realized wherever this athlete was from, half-worn tires were brand new.

> *Gratitude in America is paper thin. There aren't many other places in the world where you can still realize your dreams.*
> ✳ *Steve Welch, 2000 World #1*

Are You Really from America?

> *We shouldn't feel guilty about living in the greatest*
> *country the earth has ever seen, but*
> *we should feel responsible.*
> ✳ *Rush Limbaugh*

Patriotism means you cheer for your fellow countrymen in everything from flower growing to seed spitting, no matter what. If your country is defeated, a patriot visibly congratulates the victor, yet under the surface secretly envies and loathes his successor. Patriotism says when your country goes against your personal belief you still burn with loyalty. And when it performs grandly, you proudly puff out your chest as if the decision was all yours. A patriot stands by his country's negative examples and derives joy from the positive. Americans are frequently ridiculed, but in the history of mankind, notwithstanding individual agendas, no other country has tried any harder at doing the right thing, our freedom is emphatically valued. Our nationality is about having a voice in the choice.

> *If you don't have any enemies you don't stand*
> *for anything.*
> ✳ *Shorty Powers*

Unsure of this statement's origin, this was my thought as I watched the fireworks in Geneva over Lac Leman, as the people of Switzerland celebrated 700 years of neutrality. I was there just before America invaded Iraq and had to tolerate many comments and opinions during the tournament. Even today Americans are often accused of being imperialistic in our international relations. Pure imperialism may have existed years ago but that's a very strong accusation today. I'll be the first to admit, if we get involved we also have our own interests at heart. But if we were ruining lives while taking care of ours, I would strongly disagree. Our *accompanying intention* is to help others approach a "concept of freedom" and facilitate choices in their lives. We just happen to position ourselves within those choices.

Traveling overseas invites a myriad of feelings and feedback during dinner discussions. Most are healthy but in between the tournaments, things are different as you carefully select where your U.S.A. clothing will be worn. On occasion, I have been booed, yelled at, laughed at, spit on, stared down, pushed aside, robbed and had my clothing stolen. People seem to either really like Americans or they really don't.

There is nothing I value more than battling wearing red, white and blue, sticking out my chest and kicking some butt for the United States. In my career people would not only come to watch us play, they would come to watch us practice. During competition I always felt like I had the power of "ten Ben Franklins" and would fight as if someone was attempting to steal the Liberty Bell. Competing as an American doesn't present one rival; everyone is a rival, they all want a piece of you, which creates an additional amount of pressure and pride.

With all the censure and scrutiny of the United States, never have I ever heard of anyone switching their nationality to any other country than America. There are many different speeds but the road to America goes one way. I was in Hong Kong just before it was handed back to the Chinese, and had intimate conversations with two local citizens who were friends and entrepreneurs. Their apprehension of the transfer aroused my sympathy for them, and appreciation for home. Interestingly, the younger feared the Chinese less, while the older friend, who owned a company and had more to lose, had a higher degree of apprehension. Can you imagine going through this experience and not having any say?

The United States has been spoiled and punished, dominated and raped, immortalized and chastised; she is continuously under construction and never stays the same. She isn't a country; she's an ideal. Maybe my genealogical connection to Robert E. Lee has inflated my feelings, but concerning one's country, "Live there, support there…I don't really care where." Just like America, sometimes a stand must be made. Call me old-fashioned, call me stubborn, but please call me an American.

After we defeated Spain in the bronze medal game at the Atlanta Paralympics, a friend asked if I would give my jersey to a disabled child that loyally attended every one of our games. We had finished, it was over, it didn't matter; plus this kid's patriotism was impressive. I showed him my medal, then asked if he would like to have my jersey. He couldn't even look at me as I placed it in his outstretched hand, then he held it up to show his mom.

Four years later I attended a Blaze Sports Camp for kids in Macon, Georgia conducted by compassionate U.S.A. Quad Rugby Coach Wendy Gumbert, that was sponsored by the United States Disabled Athletes Fund. During the orientation, I noticed a very athletic kid wearing a jersey resembling our U.S.A. uniforms in Atlanta. As I wheeled up behind him, I noticed it was very worn and faded and had the name "Snow" on the back. It was mine. Initially looking for some appreciation, I started to ask if he remembered me that night at the Omni, but my better judgment emerged. There was no reason for an ego moment. The boy had benefited from the intention of the gift.

With the "pack loyalty" of a wolf, I will be a Dallas Cowboy fan forever. But when football is discussed in Europe, don't expect names like Aikman or Smith to surface. Their football is real football, which Americans call soccer.

After finishing our competition in London, "the Kuerz" and I were on our way to Rome. The French were on strike (what's new) so we were forced to cross the English Channel into Holland, then take a two-day train ride through the Italian countryside. I have never seen so many sunflowers in my life.

England was playing Italy that night in the World Cup quarterfinals and each time the train stopped more of the *loaded* British fans boarded. By the time we arrived in Milan, our car was standing-room-only. The passionate Italians were disgusted with the drunken British soccer fans. Once, a fight broke out in our car, which pushed the crowd over on top of me. It doesn't behoove a wheelchair person to get caught in the middle of a fight among a hundred able-bodied people, and especially stuffed in a train in a foreign country. I yelled, then huddled for cover, but only a quarter of them understood English anyway. Somehow I survived.

From every corner the historical statements of Rome demanded attention but the most breathtaking was the Coliseum. It quietly roared at us. At one time it was even filled with water for mock naval battles. How they kept that porous stadium filled with water,

I will never know. And to be on the same floor where the lion/Christian incidents took place was very strange.

We exchanged some money, then checked into the Catacombs, which dually served as a dormitory for nuns. The next day we drifted through the ancient tombs located under the monastery, then that evening went on an exploration run to find some food. As we walked through the streets, we noticed that the entire city seemed to be preoccupied, as if in a spooky episode of the Twilight Zone. Any verbal attempt for service invited looks as if we were from another country. *Sorry.* At one shop we could have taken anything as the owner and employees just sat at a table with their backs to us. Upon further investigation, we found the people on each street corner, and in every store and home, drawn to their television sets. In our excitement we had forgotten about the game and finally noticed that all of Rome was tuned to the World Cup soccer match. And just as it was making sense, Italy scored a goal.

Words can't compete for the emotional energy that followed. I have heard many types of cheers but never have I *felt* anything like that. In a slow roll, a huge tidal wave of energy enveloped the city as five million people, in fact the whole country, came to a crescendo of yells, whistles, horns and energy. It was as if a most horrible ruler had just been guillotined. We were caught by surprise but soon were consumed by the power. Thanks to the Italian culture, at that moment we knew patriotism. Italy won the game 1–0.

My grandfather once picked up a penny and put it into his pocket. I said, "Gampie, what did you do that for?" He said, "This will make me rich." "How can picking up a penny make you rich?" "Well now, picking up the penny won't, but the habit will."

We must make caring a choice. If we don't develop the "habit of patriotism" this property we call home will change drastically, offering some uncomfortable adjustments.

No Regrets

People experience many different opportunities in their life but not many get to compete in the Olympics, and especially from a wheelchair. I don't know how many times I've had to correct biographies or press releases, but I am an Olympian and a Paralympian.

Over the last 20 years less than 40 male wheelchair athletes have done this and only one American has ever won a silver medal.

In 1983, the Los Angeles Olympic Organizing Committee announced two exhibition races; a men's 1500-meter and women's 800-meter race, for people in wheelchairs. These inaugural events would be held in the coliseum during the 1984 Summer Games and allow the physically disabled to display their skills in the highest athletic venue in the world.

When the announcement was made, my track coach, Judy Einbinder and I made the decision to *make the attempt*. We established a trust-filled relationship, I moved to Houston and we went to work. For the next year I trained like never before, lifting weights, working diligently on the track, and averaging 100 miles a week. Many athletes from around the world were involved in similar programs, in hope of winning a medal and advocating for people with disabilities. Ask any U.S. athlete attempting to qualify for the Olympics; surviving the trials is sometimes more difficult than the actual event. There is great pressure in getting there.

At the Games for the Disabled at Hoffstra University, in New York, three Canadians, two Americans, one German, one Aussie, and one Belgian earned the right to compete in the men's event. The excitement was unbelievable as Jim Martinson and I were the Americans.

At the Olympics, we were respected as athletes, staying at the same facility, eating and living with our able-bodied counterparts and rubbing elbows with the great ones. During a lunch once I backed out of the food line and ran over Mary Lou Retton's foot. I'm sure I impressed her as I offered the savvy line of "pardon me." Then I sat at a table with "Flo Jo" and "Flo" Hyman, at which point, a huge man hidden by a hooded top with 'U.S.A. Boxing' on the front said, "Here, you left your milk at the counter." They told me his name was Holyfield. He and I were the only athletes warming up on the practice track the morning of our race. Competing as athletes with athletes was "live."

We wheeled into the Coliseum on August 11, 1984, to 80,000 cheering spectators, and the race began. At the 1000-meter point, contact between a Canadian and the Aussie sent me outside the pack, avoiding a crash. For a brief moment I considered running down Van Winkle, the Belgian, who was ahead by fifteen meters, but decided to *settle* for a chance for second place. As we came around the last turn, I tapped into the preparation and confidence Judy had worked so hard to instill and out-sprinted the rest of the field to secure the silver medal. There I was, on the Olympic medal stand in Los Angeles winning a silver medal for me, my country and for disabled folks around the world, and I was so proud.

As the Belgian National Anthem played, my heart ached as I realized that greatness had come and I had let her leave. Don't get me wrong, a silver medal in the Olympics is a fabulous accomplishment, but the problem with a silver medal is…it's silver. To this day I still carry regrets because *I didn't go for the gold medal*. I had regretfully made the decision to settle because I doubted myself. Becoming involved in comparison, for a "regret-filled" moment, I believed I didn't measure up.

Do we realize the power we have in our decisions? Will we look back on our life and wish we had done something different? Will we seriously consider past experiences in our next decision? To this day I still don't know what would have happened if I had tried.

Habla Mi Language?

The British Open Wheelchair Tennis Tournament is held in Nottingham, England each year and yes, he does exist. I saw *R. Hood* signed in the guest book of an old hotel dating to the 1190s when he was to have ridden throughout Sherwood Forest.

I had lost a tough semi-final match and was very disappointed… well, OK, I was pissed. But there's one good thing about losing in Europe…you're in Europe. Shakespeare's birthplace was located near Warwick Castle in Stratford-Upon-Avon, so a group of us *losers* hit the train.

One of the finest athletes and individuals on the tour was a Japanese player named Yumi who was with us that day. A double amputee from a construction accident, he had received a large settlement of money after his accident. Yumi was very talented in tennis but he couldn't speak a word of English.

The Japanese are extraordinary people, polite, formal, and the most gracious hosts. It is considered disrespectful if you refill your glass at a reception because it suggests they aren't attending to their guests. When the final in the Japan Open is posted for 2 p.m., unlike the Israelis who really mean 2:47 p.m. or 3:28 p.m., it means 2 p.m. But don't judge the Israelis on being "punctuality challenged," they are just interested in other things. There is a huge difference between *being stupid* and *not being interested*.

A big crowd of people boarded our train, which separated us into different cars. We were connected visually but verbally we couldn't communicate. Being a chronic nap taker, and agreeing with the "clickety-clack" of the train, Yumi drifted off to sleep while sitting up in his chair. As the train quietly pulled to a stop, we noticed that an older English couple had stopped in front of Yumi. They were attempting to put a rolled up English note into the Coke can held between his stumps. Startled, he woke up, realized what was happening, and attempted to deny the donation by moving his hands back and forth. He kept shaking his head side to side in a "No" gesture, but the English couple mistook this as pride and insisted he take the money. Realizing he couldn't properly communicate, he finally acquiesced and let the lady put the note into the can.

Looking at it from the couple's perspective, here was this poor Asian guy with no legs sleeping in a wheelchair, probably tired from working all night in some low paying job, and just trying to make it home to his wife and "seventeen children". From Yumi's perspective, here was a wealthy athlete who was just napping after flying two days to get to England, who couldn't communicate that he didn't need the money. We couldn't help but chortle.

One of the most amazing displays of communication I have ever witnessed was between blind athletes and their tethered guides during long distance running. Training early one morning in Barcelona, I had no "match play" and decided to take in some other sports, so I departed for the stadium. By pulling some strings and manipulating (of which I have no real skill), I was able to get down on the track. I really wanted to see the wheelchair racers but that day was reserved for the blind athletes, specifically the 5000-meter event. At one time I held the national record in that event and understood the strategy, so I stayed.

As the athletes came onto the track, I was absorbed in their racing mantra. Different people with different skills from different countries using different languages yet connected by fate. I immersed in their *functional diversity*. The more I watched, the more I became interested in the interaction between the visually impaired runners and their guides. Each blind athlete was connected to their guide by a small rope called a tether. The obvious considerations existed. What if the blind runner was slower or faster than the sighted runner?

How would the teams communicate since they were from different countries? Would there be room for a sprint to the end?

In Sydney there was a problem in one race because a guide had malaria, but because of the Paralympic rules, he could not be replaced. Controversy broke when the blind athlete actually led the exhausted guide around the track for the last two laps. Because of this, the duo missed a world record by a few seconds but still won the gold medal. Passing the protest, there exist varying levels of visually impaired athletes. This blind athlete could see just well enough to finish the race.

The race started with the usual pacing and jockeying, with light tactile and audio communication. As the race quickened, one by one, the pack was reduced. For the losers, the psychology that attempts to salvage a positive Paralympic memory took over. For the others though, the hunt for more was obvious, as they had done their work and expected nothing less than gold. As they banked around the last turn for the sprint to the finish, I witnessed an "eye-opening" sight. Here were five teams of athletes tethered together in full sprint with years of effort passionately captured in their *expression full* faces. Worrying about what they may look like has no value to a blind person, as first impression reactions aren't witnessed; there is no distraction. In their native tongues the sighted runners were shouting "This is it, come on, go, go, take it home!" as they sprinted.

The finish of that race was a summary of awareness, teamwork, communication and trust. In any communication there is always two interpretations, from the communicator and by the receiver. Too frequently, we feel our interpretation is correct.

Take My Seat

> *In life we meet with triumph and tragedy,*
> *and must treat the impostors the same.*
> ✳ *Rudyard Kipling*

I had just boarded a bus to return to the village at the Paralympics in Sydney. Tired, and feeling a bit sorry for myself since I had just *watched* the tennis final, I had added to my day by taking in the U.S. men's basketball game as well as the U.S. quad rugby competition. A difficult moment for me and the other 9500 fans as I did play-by-play for We Media's live video streaming, was when a fan with Tourette's Syndrome had a seizure and broke the immaculate silence during one of the points. At the top of the stands among thousands of fans and Welch and Hall in the middle of a point, can you imagine someone yelling at the top of their lungs "all of you, all of you, aaaaaaahhhhhhh, all of you, NNNOOOOOOH!" My explanation to the audience was a placation at best.

At the bus stop my melancholy was interrupted by a group of large "vertical" athletes who boarded singing a patriotic song in a language I couldn't understand. If I had not been so tired and if it hadn't been the Paralympics, I would have been very intimidated. Most of them had some type of amputation or prosthetic device but because of the severity of his injury, the last man caught my attention.

He was badly burned along both arms, and his face and his ears were melted. He was a single amputee on crutches and needed to sit so I pulled down one of the retractable seats, motioned and moved over. The words on his hat asked for my attention. They said "Coach-Bosnia-Hercogovinia Paralympic Team."

He courteously acknowledged me, turned to his teammates and said something and the team cheered again and began singing. I said, "Do you speak English?" In broken English he said, "Of course." I said, "Why is your team so happy?" He told me he was the coach of the Bosnian sitting volleyball team and that they had just defeated Korea, which placed them in the final against Iran. They were guaranteed at least a silver medal, which would be the first since the independent status of their two-year old country.

While they continued to cheer, he noticed me admiring his hat and asked if I wanted to trade. We traded hats to cheers for Bosnia and America and we also took our shirts off and exchanged right there on the bus. I asked the coach how to say "Kick Iran's Butt" in Bosnian and after a couple of recitals, yelled it out loud. The team went crazy.

This was one of those spontaneous "once-in-a-lifetime" moments that engrave an indelible indentation in the soul. As we approached the transportation mall, where all athletes must trickle through security, my curiosity again defeated my inhibition. I quietly asked, "What happened to you?" His eyes met mine as he paused and said, "You know what happened to me. I promise you I was not born this way." I said, "My country's heart pours out for you." "Thank you."

Tennis Anyone?

> *Change*
> *There were two caterpillars sitting on the ground talking. Just as a beautiful butterfly swooped right over their heads, one caterpillar said to the other, No way man, you'll never get me on one of those things.*
> ✳ *Author unknown*

The 1992 Games in Spain carried significant value because of the recent ending of the Persian Gulf War. Especially for Americans, there was always the possibility of an incident. Gathering outside the Olympic Stadium in Barcelona, over 5000 athletes and coaches prepared for one of the greatest experiences in an athlete's life. The United States team, 450 strong, had lined up to enter into a sea of 80,000 waiting fans. After hours of pre-ceremonial briefing, we finally approached the much-anticipated moment of coming though the tunnel. As I have mentioned, the best description I can offer of this moment is to imagine floating in a canoe down a river towards the sound of a rushing waterfall. The sound of thousands of cheering people is definitely a Dick Clark top ten hit.

As with a concert or a Broadway play, I love to be right up front during an opening ceremony. My mom said her favorite part of Atlanta was watching the astonishment of the athletes who had never experienced anything that grand, as they entered and momentarily drifted in awe.

Since the United States is spelled *Estados Unidos* in Spanish, we alphabetically entered the stadium under the "E's." As we waved to the thousands, our procession circled the track. Then we pulled into our designated area to watch the arrival of the others. Since the "I's" followed, Iraq soon entered the stadium. I will never forget the looks on their faces as their eyes met ours. Many years in a wheelchair affords the ability to determine the length of a person's disabled career, and clued by the recent conflict, the Iraqi athletes had not *been there* very long. Inviting deep contemplation, that moment had great solemnity as the Iraqis passed on by.

As in any good movie, the director manipulates emotion by timing a high after a low. Life, the greatest movie of all, presented its version, because the second letter after "I" was "K." The Kuwaitis proudly entered to cheers and praise and as they noticed us they vociferously rejoiced by yelling, "America, Yeah, America."

The roller coaster of emotion is difficult to describe during the passing of those two countries. I was involved in anger, guilt, compassion, joy and gratitude, all in about fifteen minutes. As the ceremony ended, we began to mingle and the societal molds of acceptability were dissolved into a tapestry of culture and ethnic celebration. Later I had the experience of being together with an Iraqi and Kuwaiti as we looked into each other's eyes, full knowing the participation of each other's culture. Here were three athletes from three conflicting nations after a major war, in harmonious dialogue.

I know its more complicated than this, but I can't help but think if the leaders of these nations had played tennis one afternoon and met each other's families, would we have still experienced the devastation of the Persian Gulf War? With a palatable awareness of gratitude, we embraced, conversed and exchanged.

First Impressions

A reporter just before going to Sydney, who seemed very distracted, was interviewing me. Though I was attending my fourth Paralympic competition, this guy wasn't reacting to my accomplishments like I thought he ought to be. While he was working on some notes, the cameraman said, "He's really doing a great job today...considering." Frustrated by my hurt ego, I said "Considering what?" "His father died this morning."

Even though Belgium is considered a step-child to Holland and France, I've never understood this and have always had a great time there. One of my favorite things to do in Belgium is to go to Rue de Bousher (the street of the butcher), and eat moules (mussels) at the 100-year-old restaurant, Chez Leon. For a Texan, dipping bread in the residual juices of a bucket of steamed mussels is to die for.

One night Greg Gibbens ate two pots of the shellfish and experienced diarrhea, the *paraplegia demon*. We can be very supportive in the wheelchair world, yet within our fraternity exists punishing insensitivity. Greg and his partner had to play doubles against the great Mick Connell and me. Since the combination of diarrhea and paraplegia demands its victim to sit still, we decided to *push the demon*. By bombarding Greg with shots that forced him to extend, we might be lucky enough to get a reaction. To our delight Greg only lasted three games before leaving the court to *relieve us all*.

Leaving the statue of Manneken Pis, we were touring the park district of Brussels with the father of the tournament director, who was a retired World War II veteran. We weren't too excited about spending the day with this older gentleman, but on his own time he had agreed to take us into the city. We were leisurely strolling through the City Museum area when a tractor-trailer pulled up carrying a huge German Panzer tank. As we rambled by, the loudest engine I have ever heard violated the serenity of the park. The sound froze everyone. We stopped, turned and watched as they began to drive the tank off the tractor-trailer. Then he quietly spoke.

He informed us that the Panzer was the same type of tank that ran through the park forty-five years before. Without consideration, the tanks destroyed Brussels and ruined people's lives, and he had not heard that sound in that place since. We tried to understand the terror and fear as he told a story of how he once buried himself to avoid being killed. I saw incredible depth in his face as he, and many others around the park, mentally reminisced. Having no prior knowledge of his experiences, for the rest of the day I looked at him differently.

We all have breath taking and heart-aching experiences that aren't worn like clothing for others to see yet are indelibly stamped into our being. They affect how we interact with the people around us. We never truly know a person when we meet them and sometimes don't even know him after spending intimate time. Our experiences mold us, contributing to our thoughts, decisions and actions. What's sad is that we can't immediately occupy unconditional respect for all people regardless of what *we think we know*.

Randy and Santa Claus in 1961.
Is that a Roho cushion?

Dorothy and Randy McElhone (grandparents)

MC and Hazel Snow (grandparents)

Sisters Becca, Jenny, Molly, Mom, Randy, Tom (stepfather) and little sis' Lee

Sisters and their families, with Tom and Rose Snow (stepmom) at Padre Island

Great-grandfather Patrick
Henry McElhone, 1942

Randy at Apacheland
Tennis Camp, Tyler, 1975

Tractor on which injury occurred, 1975

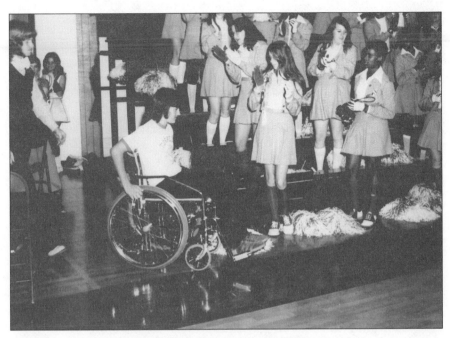

Just after injury at Terrell High School pep rally, 1977

Shorty Powers, Randy, and Greg Gibbens in Las Vegas, 1984

Jim Moortgat, Bal and
Marcha Moore, Randy,
and Frank Burns

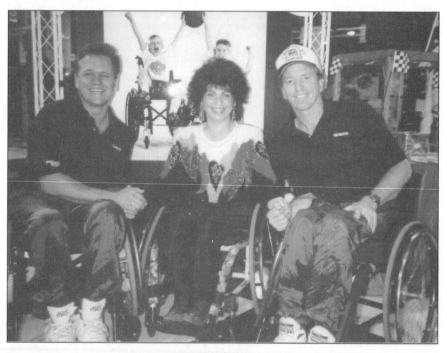

Randy, Marilyn Hamilton, and David Kiley

After winning German Open over Laurent Giamartini, 1992. He was not happy!

Signing autographs after gold medal win in Barcelona

With Dr. Bal Moore
after winning
second gold medal
in Barcelona

Showing off one of the 18 wheel trucks used to promote the Atlanta
Paralympics in 1996

Participating in 1500 meter race in Olympics in Los Angeles and winning silver medal (Photographer: Curt Beamer. Copyright © by *Sports N Spokes Magazine*. Reprinted by permission.)

Fishing guru and good friend Dub Gibbens in Golden Meadow

At President's Council for Physical Fitness with President Bush, 1991

Receiving the Paralympic torch from President Clinton in Washington, 1996

Australian player and friend Mick Connell, Gene Wilder, Ivan Lendl, and Randy at exhibition in 1991

Randy, John McEnroe and Steve Welch at Nuveen Tennis in Florida

Christopher Reeve at National Paralysis Foundation Gala in Dallas

Opening Ceremonies at Atlanta Paralympics...can you find Randy?

Chapter Thirteen

Our Future

The quickest way off the pity potty is to talk to a kid.
✳ *Liz Morrison*

Never Give Up

I have witnessed hundreds of examples of individuals who have been subjected to incredible adversity and most have responded with uncommon valor. But the following story has significant impact.

My trip to Africa exposed me to change, survival and corruption. I had been touted as the world champion that would tour South Africa and teach tennis and encourage people to dream. Out of my protective environment, I was shocked to witness such struggle. I wasn't allowed to leave the Hyatt in downtown Johannesburg because I was told I would certainly be mugged and possibly killed. The only way I could go was if I was accompanied by one of the armed guards from the lobby. One day I returned from teaching and discovered that my room had been robbed of some clothing and after reporting the incident, the manager said, "I will fire the employee if you want, but she steals a lot less than the others. May I just replace your items?"

The situation stems from scathing lifestyle differences without blame for either side. Since everyone there is a native, they are all South Africans and in my opinion, are entitled to be there. Yet the contrast in culture is so glaring, a resolution may not be possible for years. Promised free health care and housing, the tribal blacks were lured to the cities, but the social system couldn't meet its promises. Hundreds of thousands of families packed their belongings and moved to the metropolis areas but when they arrived there wasn't any work or shelter. Needing a place to live, they settled on land outside "Joburg" and the other larger cities in makeshift homes. I toured a shantytown called Soweto and was shocked to find 50,000 people without running water or electricity.

Our sports camp invited all kids, regardless of color. With Winnie Mandella in attendance, the camp did not discriminate as kids were bused in from all over the city. The luxury of discrimination didn't exist within our ethnography. As we began the camp we were asked to participate in an opening ceremony highlighted by a wheelchair tennis exhibition. Intending to impress the kids, I hit the first ball hard but it went into the crowd. All of a sudden a little hand appeared and caught the 90-mph serve. Relieved, we went on and played the exhibition.

After the ceremony and the sponsor speeches, I went to find the kid with "incredible eye-hand coordination." I located him among the sea of children and reached down to pull his chair towards me. Startled, I discovered he wasn't in a wheelchair, he was in an office chair. At first I thought the kid was joking around, probably something I would do? But I learned he was using the office chair for the camp. In fact there were several kids in office chairs and a few in wheelbarrows.

I bring you this story with a heavy heart. I delivered tennis balls to all kinds of kids throughout the camp, using many different types of mobility bases. Some even had wooden parts on their chairs. With unbreakable attitudes, these kids didn't care about what other people thought or who had the better chair…they just wanted to participate, to hit balls and have fun…they weren't even aware of their misfortune. I was making more of an issue of it than they were.

It took me a long time but over the years I have been able to find God's message here. Initially intending to make a difference in their life, it was inverted as they made a huge difference in my life. This story isn't about feeling sorry for these children. They don't feel sorry for themselves. Having a bad day is part of being human. This story is about not giving up. When it comes to quitting, no matter what is happening in our lives—*we don't cave in*. To *push forward* is inherent in our unwavering yet flexible resiliency. Our only challenge is to make sure we don't forget it!

A Weakness Is a Strength

I had just finished a quick lunch of spaghetti and marinara sauce and was on my way back to work when I remembered I had an appointment with my dentist. Why we pick up around the house before company, clean out the car before going to the car wash, or brush our teeth before going to the dentist, I don't know, but I spent the remaining driving time picking out pasta particles. I guess I wanted Dr. Joe to *think I was perfect*. By the way, Dr. Joe is a paraplegic swimmer who competed in the 1988 and 1992 Paralympics.

The check-up revealed that, because of my leg pains, I was gritting my teeth so Dr. Joe recommended a mouthpiece to be worn for protection. Just like every other American, I was in a hurry so I encouraged him to quickly do what was necessary. Here is a test for you. You know you are going too fast in life if after placing something in the microwave for three minutes, you stop the timer with ten seconds left because you "want it now."

As he left the room, his technical assistant came in and introduced herself as Erin. She told me she was in high school and in a work study program. She began to explain the procedure and at a moment that was very important to her she said, "Now be very careful, this material could squirt down your throat and stimulate your gag reflex." I said "Erin, I have won the U.S. Open ten times and met three presidents, I am a mental giant, it's all mind control, I will not throw up." She relaxed and said, "Good, because I have a strong gag reflex and if you throw up, I'll throw up."

Thinking this was way too much information, I pitied her. She proceeded to mix the material and as soon as I bit down, that stuff shot right back, hung in my throat and stimulated an uncontrollable urge. Thinking "mind control, mind control," I couldn't help myself and lost my lunch, the mouthpiece and any hope of salvaging humility. As I readjusted, I glanced up at Erin who was slowly backing up as her face was turning white. Suddenly she fulfilled her promise and joined me with her own "party," then ran out of the room. As Dr. Joe came back into the office and reinforced the fact that the material could stimulate the gag reflex, in typical victim fashion I said, "I wish she would have told me that." Sometimes admitting a weakness is a strength.

> *There are three things that are very hard...*
> *steel, a diamond, and to know one's self.*
> ✳ *Benjamin Franklin*

Future Events Appearing Real

> *If there is fear in considering an important decision in life, doesn't that indicate it's what we are suppose to do?*
> ✳ *Canadian wheelchair basketball coach Mike Frogley*

No nepotism here, my four-year-old nephew Joseph, is absolutely the cutest boy ever. I invite you to meet this kid before I'm asked to defend my statement. Currently, he is in a serious Batman portrayal, while my concurrent imitation is none other than Superman. No, I don't think he knows about Christopher Reeve.

A few Sundays ago, my sister and her family were attending church. As the priest entered, entertainingly, Joseph said out loud, "There He is, there He is." Later, as my sister received communion and began accompanying Joseph back to the pew, he loudly exclaimed, "Hey, wait, I want one." Everyone giggled. After removing another communion, Father leaned down to hand it to Joseph, but he recoiled and inquired "Oh, is it too spicy?" The entire congregation laughed in delight. He knows enough about the world to innocently inquire as to why, yet doesn't own the adult inhibitors that can "ruin the ride." I wish I were more like him.

Joseph, "PaPa," and I were surrounded by Christmas decorations in the living room of "PaPa's" house. Rose, my stepmom, is the "Queen of Festivity," providing enthusiasm and decoration for all holidays, birthdays and family ceremonies. If there are angels among us, she is one.

While playing with an antique Santa Claus, Joseph knocked him off the table, which broke off one of his ceramic arms. I said, "Oooohhhh, Joseph, you're in trouble, go hide, go hide." Also in jest, my Dad said, "Grammy is going to be mad." Staring at both of us and now laden with fear, Joseph paused for a moment, then ran out of the room yelling "Grammy, Grammy...I broke the Santa Claus."

Betrayed of our wise advice, dad and I just looked at each other. What a lesson for two veteran "skaters." Our strategy represented how most respond when faced with something that *appears* to be dreadful. Certainly manufacturing the most fear possible, then creating a need to run and hide has some value (like what), but Joseph stuck our distortion right down our throats.

Face your fears as quickly as possible and the rest is like a ride in the "Batmobile." In celebration of the refreshing dialect of Australia, "good on ya, Batman."

> *In order to become healthy, we must embrace what we fear the most.*
>
> ✳ *Steven Covey*, The 7 Habits of Highly Effective People

Core Beliefs

Nancy was a very interested and adroit counselor at Central Texas Treatment Center. A windfall of resource, she reinforced that the most important ingredient in dealing with childhood demons and getting healthy was that we know our core beliefs.

Core beliefs are the indelible messages that are impressed upon us during our first few years as human beings. Whether positive or negative, this *first recording* can be re-recorded, but the initial message is never erased. If we learned insecurity, fear or neglect, they would base our being. In contrast, if we were loved and told we were champions, this positive message would influence us in whatever we did. It all comes back to core beliefs, the first recording on our brain at the impressionable age. If you seek approval from or still fear a parent, if you have a resounding message of inadequacy, or if you are confident no matter what happens, you know what I mean. To keep from hearing a negative *first recording* we must continuously record over it. It's called "working on our selves." But core beliefs are *indelibly stamped*.

I know I sound like Dr. Laura here but kids will only be at this impressionable age for a short time. During this "fresh tape," make sure that your children are aware that they are loved, are able to learn on their own and that mistakes are OK as long as they learn from them. Kids at that core belief age must know they measure up, no matter what. A child will re-play an "I love you" message all day long.

One of my godchildren is being raised in the unique and rewarding environment of parents from different countries. Karin and

Mick are from Holland and Australia, respectively, and in my opinion they provide a very healthy home. After experiencing the blessing of having a son, they decided to repeat the process, and three years later, Danique was welcomed into the world.

When I was world # 1, my priority was always to win, but the body will let one know when it is time to "step down from Olympus." There won't be any doubt. The benefits of retirement are, you don't have to put the effort into attempting to win anymore and past accomplishments get better every day. Living with a different perspective, my new priority became to see my friends and spend time with their kids. Piggy-backing the Dutch Open Wheelchair Tennis Championships, I was able to visit my Godchild Kai and his sister, Danique.

Taking Danique with us one afternoon, Mick and I wheeled throughout the little community of which they lived and ended up going to the bank to exchange some money. While we were waiting in line, Danique began to fall asleep. When a three-year old falls asleep, they are out for the count, a sack of potatoes, in the land of Orpheus. Mick said, "Do you think you can you carry her home?" I said, "Sure, Mick." I placed Danique on my lap and started out the door, but she kept slipping to either side, causing me to wheel with one hand and hold her with the other. Before we got to the door, Mick produced a Velcro strap, placed it around us and secured her to me. This worked for awhile but as we continued down the road, her head started rolling from side to side like someone asleep on an airplane, so I held it under my chin. We wheeled the remaining distance with many passers by acknowledging our procession with smiles.

Now I know Danique was sound asleep, but there is a significant lesson here of trust. In life, we do the best we can with what we have, but when it doesn't go our way, sometimes we force our will. Rather than attempting to control people, places and things, I am reminded that we must do our best, then *trust that life will work out*. It's difficult but if we can incorporate a little more trust in our lives, our faith will be strengthened.

1. Children are not pets.

2. The life they actually live and the life you perceive them to be living is not the same.

3. Don't take what children do too personally.

4. Don't keep scorecards. A short memory is suggested.

5. Dirt and mess are a breeding ground for well-being.

6. Stay out of their rooms after puberty.

7. Stay out of their friendships and love life unless invited in.

8. Don't worry that they never listen to you. Worry that they are watching you.

9. Learn from them, they have much to teach you.

10. Love them long but let them go early.

You will never really know what kind of parent you were. And you will worry about this and them as long as you live. But when your children have children and you watch what they do, you will have your answer.
✳ *Author unknown.*

Respond to Ability

According to the Department of Labor, disabled workers have less absenteeism than their able-bodied coworkers. Once the acceptance process has been realized, with renewed responsibility, the person with a disability welcomes the opportunity to work and will attend and participate. As America continues to mistake "privileges for principles," the example of a little girl with cerebral palsy made it very clear to me what responsibility means.

Taylor was a participant in our wheelchair sports program in Birmingham. She wasn't very talented yet she truly benefited from the social and physical parts of the program. She loved Super Sports Saturday and didn't miss an event.

After speaking to the kids about my participation in the Olympic exhibition, I showed a video of our race. Usually talkative, Taylor was very quiet during the discussion period. As the kids began to trickle back into the gym for the afternoon activities, Taylor waited for a private moment, then came up to me and said, "Coach Snow, may I ask you a question?" "Sure Taylor, what is it?" "Weren't you embarrassed to be in front of all those people?" I was caught off guard by her inquiry. Embarrassed, was I embarrassed to be in front of 80,000 screaming, sport-appreciative fans, cheering me around the track? I had made many sacrifices and worked extremely hard to get right there. That was exactly where I wanted to be. I would rather have been there than anywhere in the world. Her question enlightened me as to our individual perceptions and beliefs, and our responsibility.

Once I was sitting with about 25 wheelchair tennis players in a tennis club in Holland as a guy with cerebral palsy walked between us. He had the usual spastic CP gait, however he skillfully guided himself through the chairs and tables without touching a single one. My friend Brenka commented, "Look at him, you and I see him as competently skilled, but if he were in a club filled with able-bodied people, he would stand out severely."

Our perceptions form our beliefs, which influence our behaviors. These experiences create filters, which form *what we think we know*. Taylor was using all of her available information to form her own ideas. This little girl's life was filled with being stared at, teased and patronized to the point of being imprisoned by perceived inadequacy and inability. To her, being in front of thousands of people in a wheelchair represented something awful, which contradicted my paradigm of spending four hours each day in my track chair trying to get to that exact place. Living unaware of another perspective, she would always feel oppressed. I felt my responsibility was to expose her to a broader way of thinking so at least she would have the *choice* of making a more informed decision.

Imagine competing in the Olympics for America as a black athlete in the late 60s. Traveling in the backs of buses, using different dressing- and bath-rooms, and living under civil oppression was counter to lining up, side by side, with Anglo brethren to compete for Yankee pride. I love the story of Juan Carlos and Tommy James who after donning black gloves held their fists high in the air during the 200-meter medal ceremony at the Olympics in Mexico City in 1968. I've seen the interviews from that time; these athletes didn't want to champion any cause or risk losing their medals by participating in a highly controversial demonstration, *yet was it their responsibility?* This is quite different from the arrogance of the 4 x 100-meter sprinters who acted without responsibility for *anything* on the medal stand in Sydney.

Should Jesse Owens have dipped the flag in Berlin? Should Arther Ashe have played in, and won the U.S. Open in 1968?

Should first time Boston Marathon wheelchair racer Bob Hall have said back in 1977, "You're right. Wheelchair athletes can't do the distance and shouldn't be in this race."

We Are in Peril

Within the disabled communities around the world, I have witnessed "adaptation incredible." Lip reading by a person who is hearing-impaired can't help but catch an onlooker's attention. Consider the degree of difficulty a person with severe cerebral palsy experiences during attainment of a doctorate, when reading is next to impossible. And the beak of a parrot functions as a hand, just as the mouth of a spinal cord injury. What would Charles Darwin say about the accommodating ability of the contemporary disabled? I am confident he would be impressed.

Fueled by options, the key to adapting is to focus on the little steps of progress rather than the end result. The quadriplegics in rehab back at Craig hospital amazed me. Because they had difficulty operating the call button to the nurse's station from their beds, a past patient developed a rubber ball with a mercury sensor inside. At night, the ball would be suspended half a centimeter above the patient's mouth. If the ball were moved ever so slightly the mercury would contact the sensor and engage the call button.

My situation is not as challenging or *potentially rewarding* as a quadriplegic's, but in the development of "survival psychology," challengers fall in love with problem solving. Over time, it changes from "I can't do this" to "how am I going to do this?" My neighbor, Mr. Earl Stephens and I adapted my riding lawn mower with a hand-controlled device that allowed me to independently cut the grass. I was very proud of the control and mowed my lawn way too frequently. Not having mowed grass since my injury, I still get great pleasure out of mowing because it's a mindless activity with visible results, the ultimate therapy for men. But risk taking has its price. Carried away in the "spirit of mowing," I once had to scoot 150 feet across ant beds and stickers back to my wheelchair because I forgot to fill my mower up with gas. Living in the country at the time, I was grateful that a pack of dogs didn't "happen by" while I was scooting. An explanation of the possible scenarios isn't necessary. But the benefits of risk taking usually outweigh the costs incurred. Considering adaptation, as the character played by Jeff Goldblum in *Jurassic Park* said about the "female only" dinosaurs reproducing, "Life will find a way."

There is no better example of adapting than that of nine-year-old spina bifida track star April. Many of the kids we recruited for our track program had never participated in any type of sport. Getting them to come to the track was the hard part. Once they showed up and received their track chair, truancy was not a problem. Tuesday night was reserved for track practice. We would work on starts, stroke technique and drafting. And we would talk about body image, sportsmanship and being a competitor. The big day would be the regional meet where our kids would participate in their first true competition, attempting to qualify for Junior Nationals.

The day finally arrived, as April's first race was the 100-meter event. She was precious at the starting line with her gloves taped up, her hair pulled back into a single pony tail, her racing glasses on and her track jersey tucked in. She had prepared for greatness. As the starter yelled out, "On your mark," we were so proud to see her execute what she had practiced for months, placing the front wheels of her racing chair up to the line. The starter then said "Get set" and raised his pistol high in the air.

Suddenly, as April saw the gun, she took her hands off the hand rims and placed her gloved fingers in her ears. After the gun was fired, she quickly put her hands back down on the hand rims and pushed all the way to the finish line beating the other kids and winning the event. Her mom was so ecstatic, she gave us a sprint exhibition of her own, running all the way down the track to congratulate her daughter. As the timers were sorting and documenting, my name was announced over the loud speaker so I headed to the official's table. Once there, I was shocked with the news that April had been disqualified.

Disqualifying a nine-year-old spina bifida girl from her first race could be devastating but April had violated one of the common rules of track. Once an athlete is at the starting line, they must remain motionless until the gun is fired. April didn't like guns and by covering her ears to avoid the loud pop she had disqualified herself. Without any empathy from the judges in overturning their decision, I turned my attention towards April, attempting to explain to her that it was only a starter's pistol and that it didn't have any bullets. Steadfast, she said, "I don't like *any* guns."

As I returned to the officials to persuade them to see the bigger picture, April wheeled up and said, "Coach Snow, may I start with my fingers in my ears?" I didn't know the answer. After a short conference, the head official told me, "As long as she doesn't move after she is called to the line, she can have her hands in the air if she desires."

The next race for April was the 200-meters. In anticipation, our entire team watched as the starter called out, "Runners to your mark." Here was track star April, on the starter's line, with her gloved fingers sticking into her ears. Of the eight young racers, she was the only athlete in this position, but she was as serious as Marion Jones as the starter said, "Get set"..."POW!"

April won the 200-meter event and then the 400-meter race and qualified to go to San Jose, California, for the Junior Nationals and her first airplane ride ever.

> *If we aren't changing we are in peril. Figure it out!*
> ✳ *Mike Haynes*

Forget Me Not

Even today Mary can't explain the disembodied voice she heard while changing her son's diapers that sunny morning in 1986. One moment she was carefully lifting his chubby little legs and sliding a diaper in place, making mommy faces and cooing noises, happier than she thought possible. Then, on the phone, came her doctor calling with the news of her son's condition. She reacted viscerally, bursting into tears. Stepping away from the table, not wanting to scare her son, it was a haunting moment that stayed with her a long time. Finally, it faded.

Five years later, she sat on a stool in her kitchen in South Austin, waiting for, but dreading the phone call that would tell her whether the part of her son's brain, that controlled coordination, was atrophying. "I'm sorry," the radiologist said, as Mary answered the call. Flailing about the kitchen, banging on walls, she cursed a disease she could barely pronounce that was threatening her precious child, who slept peacefully in his room down the hall. The diagnosis? Ataxia-telangiectasia, or A-T, a rare genetic disorder with no treatment, much less a cure.

Patrick was everything they wanted; a brother for Erica (who had been waiting two years for a sibling), a sweet, towheaded kid fascinated by Ninja Turtles and Batman and whatever superhero was popular at the time. Always shy, he had to be coaxed out of his mom's lap to play groups, using the extra time to size up his surroundings. As researchers dipped their toes into his ocean of a disease, Patrick continued his daily worship of superheroes. And even though his balance was getting worse, he loved motion, whether chasing Bunny, his pet rabbit, or playing kickball with his friends.

Patrick navigated his way around school and home pretty well until he grew taller. Then stairs and uneven surfaces caused trouble. His family was always there to hold his hand, but since he was eleven and seeking independence, they got a balance dog, a Golden Retriever/Lab mix named "Bean." Bean became a constant companion, a buddy, always at Patrick's side when he needed someone to lean on. They went to the movies and malls and doctor's offices.

There was so much to celebrate on Patrick's 14th birthday. "Chemo" was over and he was in remission. In April though, the cancer returned, or maybe it never really went away. A bone marrow transplant was considered. "I want to do it and I don't want to talk about it anymore," Patrick told his family. Before going to Houston for the transplant, Patrick and his family took a Make-A-Wish trip to Walt Disney World. Sitting by the airplane window, looking at the clouds, he talked to his mom about heaven: "I want to go there. I think it's up there in a bunch of clouds, and there is a hole in the bottom layer you can look down and see the city. And you can step on one of the lower clouds and go down to Earth to watch over someone, someone you love, someone who needs you."

Patrick died on August 15 with Mary and Erica cradling his head in their arms. One of the most difficult questions He will have to answer is why do some children go before their parents? Children like Patrick, whose lives are short and sometimes difficult to watch, touch us all, whether we know it or not. Patrick will always be remembered, not for a meaningless death, but for a meaningful life.

What may seem simple and time-compressed on this page, was a lengthy and traumatic ordeal for this family. In speaking with

131

Mary I learned that Bean, suffering from separation anxiety, for months went into Patrick's room, picked up one of his shoes and brought it to her. In memory of how Patrick bravely lived his life and unconditionally loved his family, I tell this story to remind us of what really matters.

Will we be missed when we are gone? Certainly, in our memories and our behaviors, loved ones live forever. But all of us will leave the Earth someday and 100 years from now, who will know you? What we do right now and how we affect the people around us is what counts.

Top 10 Things Learned From Patrick's Life

1. It's all about love.

2. Loving unconditionally is more powerful than money or position.

3. "I would haves" and "I wills" don't count; how we behave right now is all that matters.

4. There are some wonderful books written about life after life, spirituality and God. Seek them out.

5. We all have a story about someone we have loved and lost, and our loved ones connect us all.

6. Spirituality is loving and giving, and has nothing to do with four walls.

7. We are not human beings on a spiritual path, but spiritual beings on a human path.

8. Relationships can be healed.

9. Disney World is magic.

10. Love survives death.

Excerpts from this story were taken from an article printed in the treAT Newsletter about Patrick written by Janet Wilson. For more information on ataxia-telangiectasia, please see www.treat-at.org.

Chapter Fourteen

Spinnakers

Good friends are like spinnakers. Stored away most of the time, when they are called upon, they fill our lives with color and power. They are unconditional.

✳ *Jenny Sperry*

Tools

I love the history surrounding the rivers in the Texas hill country. The stories of the legendary Comanches are especially intriguing as they roamed the Llano Estacado up until the late 1800s. I believe they are still in the hills above the San Saba River near the Presidio De San Saba, which was settled in 1757. Established by Spanish soldiers before the Alamo, the Presidio was overrun by Indian warriors who concealed their weapons under their clothing. Every once in awhile high on the bluff above the river *I think* I catch a glimpse of one of those warriors quietly navigating his horse through groves of mesquites still looking for his clan. I often wish I was alive then, watching with the eyes of an Indian, so I would know what they knew. Maybe I was.

Without a doubt, the San Saba is a great place to fish yet fishing any riverbank from a wheelchair is arduous at best. Not only is it tough to maneuver along the bank but it's very hard to reach good spots, land fish and untangle your line.

Thinking that it might help my access, I endured the initial inconvenience it took to ask for help in loading my kayak and brought it to the river. I situated my boat near a stable transfer place where I could enter the water. It took some time but once I was in the boat, I freely paddled and fished the river while my stepfather was indentured to the bank. Reminiscing, I was enlightened by the liberty afforded me from the use of this simple tool. It was a hassle to ask for help, but once there, the benefit far outweighed the inconvenience, as I was able to access many places that Tom was not able to reach. My fishing experience would have been completely different had I not used the tool.

Clay courts challenge wheelchair tennis players. Not only is traction fickle, the wheels create grooves that contribute to very unpredictable bounces during play. The best antidote is to practice copiously so the anticipatory skills are over-developed.

Bal Moore and I had just finished a two-hour workout at the tennis center in Barcelona and were attempting to return to the village. While waiting on transportation, we wandered into a huge building next to the tennis center and stumbled onto an entry tunnel leading to a large gym. In a strident fashion, we were talking loudly as we neared the entry. Suddenly a finger pushed through the curtain followed by a scolding usher, his lips uttering a "sssssshhhh." Creeping through the curtain, we noticed 3 crouching athletes positioned at either end of the gym, guarding a rectangular goal taped off on the floor. On their hands and knees, the 6 athletes were involved in goal ball, which is a sport for the blind. Looking up we noticed this match was being played in front of 6,000 fans.

We instantly became aware of why the usher was so stern in his chiding. *Listening* was mandatory for the performance of their team. These athletes needed complete silence in order to compete and by speaking loudly, we were denying them of their most precious tool. A member of one team would quietly move to the edge of the playing floor, athletically shoot the ball with a spin, then wait as the three athletes at the other end would listen, locate the path of the ball and attempt to stop it. The quicker they *heard* where the ball was being rolled, the quicker they could strategically position themselves to retrieve it. Watching for hours, we missed our bus.

> *A tool can be a person, cooperation or a piece of equipment. They are varied and carry unique significance as to their meaning and function.*
> ✳ *U.S. Open finalist Mark Hamman*

Better Be Changin'

> *What we get from life, we can make a living. What we give, we can make a life.*
> ✳ *Sculptured script at the site of the 1968 World's Fair in Flushing, New York*

Turning her accident around to champion the cause for thousands of others, Marilyn is one of the most dynamic individuals on the planet. Living in the foothills of the Sierra Nevada Mountains, she and her hang gliding friends cherished every flying moment, hauling their "wings" up beyond Clovis, California, and lifting off into the upland thermals. Immersed in their sport, they even designed and manufactured their own gliders.

As with any high-risk sport, on some days the benefit doesn't offset the cost, and on this day, the cost would be at a premium. Running through the usual checklist, Marilyn waited for her instinct to approve and with the next gust, committed to the sky. Her systems immediately told her something was wrong, as she never gained control of her craft. She tumbled one hundred and fifty feet down the fall line of the mountain. The impact broke her back and left her permanently paralyzed from the waist down. She would be changed forever.

While in rehabilitation, she and her friends intuitively noticed that the tubing used in her dinosaur wheelchair was the same diameter as their hang gliders. After her discharge from the hospital, this seemingly insignificant spark sent the triad into their hang gliding manufacturing facility (a garage) to challenge the existing paradigms of how wheelchairs were made. Using innovative materials, which included extruded aluminum and sailcloth, the first year they built three different wheelchairs for Marilyn. With a great deal of interest among the disabled community over this new chair, they incorporated the following year and began selling to the public, retailing several thousand dollars worth of product.

Because of its innovative technology, this much-needed wheelchair revolutionized the way people with disabilities were perceived and functioned, and it became a regional hit. They established national distribution by aligning with a network of medical vendors, while continuing to be innovative in their research and development. By the fifth year, gross sales of Quickie Designs was in the million-dollar mark and the company was purchased by Sunrise Medical for a large sum.

Peeling back the layers, life-changing events reveal who the person truly is. Leadership comes from the inside. Just as a glider provides freedom for its user, with her motto, "If you can't stand up, stand out," Marilyn turned a challenge into an opportunity. I have had the benefit of spending some of my precious time here on earth as Marilyn's friend. Working together at Quickie Designs, I have frequently asked her about competition from a manufacturing perspective, international athletics and life in general. In a statement that will be with me forever she said, "Whether leading or following, you better be changing."

> *Each day the lion gets up in the morning, looks out over the Serengeti, and knows it must run faster than the gazelle or it will starve. And each day the gazelle gets up, looks out over the Serengeti and knows it must run faster than the lion or it will be eaten. The point isn't whether you are a lion or a gazelle, but when the sun comes up—you better be running.*
> ✳ *African Proverb*

The Keys to the Lights

Greg Gibbens was not born with the talent of Andre Agassi, but he definitely had his drive. Injured when his jeep was run off the road, which caused his vehicle to roll several times, the accident left him a paraplegic. I played tennis against Greg many times and although he was determined and a student of Dr. Bal Moore, I questioned whether he held the adeptness to win the U.S. Open.

Greg's plan to win at "the show" involved hitting on his own two hours a day, training with the Jefferson State able-bodied tennis team and private sessions with Dr. Moore in the evening. He was definitely hitting a lot of balls. But as the championships drew near, Greg felt he wasn't getting enough training and asked Bal for more time. Because he was teaching college classes, coaching his own tennis team and conducting private lessons, Bal just couldn't offer Greg any more attention. There wasn't enough daylight in the day. As they faced the daylight dilemma, they came up with an idea that truly defines what it takes to be a champion.

Bal approached Dale Clark, the Director of Tennis at Pine Tree Country Club and during the conversation asked him for the keys to the lights of the courts. Dale said, "Bal, the lights come on at seven p.m. and are on till ten. I'll schedule you a court anytime, you can train all you want." Bal said, "Dale, I don't need the lights on at night, I need the keys so I can turn the lights on in the morning. We have to hit from five to seven a.m." For 3 months Greg and Bal hit in the early morning hours while every other wheelchair tennis player in America slept.

I have coached tennis for twenty years and Bal twice that, and never have we ever heard of anyone training under the lights before the sun comes up. Of all the answers I have attempted to provide wheelchair tennis players in the world as to what it takes, what Greg and Bal did is the answer. As simple as it may sound, you have to do the work.

The morning of the final of the U.S. Open at the Racket Club of Irvine, Greg was preparing with Coach Moore when a little piece of paper fluttered out of the sky and landed on their court. Acknowledging the paper, Bal noticed it was a burned page of the Bible with a verse that read, "You will go to the mountain top." Greg didn't say anything more after Bal showed him the paper. Greg came out *en fuego*, won the first nine games and captured the U.S. Open Championship 6–0, 6–2. After the match, Greg asked Bal for the burnt Bible verse but when Bal looked in his pocket, it was gone.

If you want to be successful, certainly money and talent will help, but nothing will insure your success any more than getting *the keys to the lights.*

The Utilitarian

> *How a person masters his fate is more important than what that fate is.*
> ✳ *Wilhelm von Humboldt*

Why don't we appreciate it while we still have it? We all take things for granted, it's human. Once it's gone though, whether a job, a person, or our legs, it's painful to look back and *know* that what we had was valuable.

In my motivational speeches, I talk about the "Challenger Pathway," which states it's our life *challenges* that reveal our *strengths*. From our revealed *strengths* we identify our *options*. From here we develop a *vision*, and in the pursuance of our *vision*, as Aristotle said, we "realize our essence." Leadership is learning to make the best with available resources.

As I have previously chronicled, once the shock and shame are eliminated, a person who has experienced an accident hopes to start their life over, but often it's in a complete new body with a whole new set of rules. From walking down the street to lying paralyzed in a hospital bed, withdrawing every ounce from what remains is necessary to again find a quality of life. This is the definition of utilitarian.

David van Cleave was an able-bodied basketball star at the University of Nevada. Being 6'7" has wonderful advantages in life, especially as a college basketball player or a future pro volleyball player, but not in being paralyzed from the neck down. Walking to a college dance one night, a carload of kids who were drinking slammed into him, hurling him to the ground and breaking his neck at the fourth and fifth cervical vertebrae. David would now have to learn a different way of carrying out all activities of daily living.

Rather than caving in to what most would call a "quality of life" ending event, David took on the challenge and focused on the things he could still do and *pushed forward* with "adjusted vision." Through trial and error, he became self-sufficient in daily living skills, re-entered the workforce as a school teacher and basketball coach and even found a way to compete.

After seeing an article in *Sports N Spokes Magazine*, he optimistically purchased a tennis racket, but unsure of himself, kept it in his closet for several months. Over time he developed an orthotic device to help him hold the racket in his hand, then began redeveloping the atrophied muscles in his arms. He then ventured out onto the courts, took lessons, watched the top players and read everything he could find on the sport. Today, he tours the country playing tennis and carries a high ranking in the Quad Division. Anticipating at an incredible level, he combines the difficult task of maneuvering a power chair and generating enough force to strike the ball over the net. How can I communicate to you the skill involved here? What he does with what he has is athleticism that every athlete in the world should envy.

The development of adapting requires fearless persistence, which becomes a "philosophy of living." Quadriplegics truly represent utilitarian life, adapting, maximizing strengths, and squeezing the most out of limited physical resource. The problem-solving David experiences, carrying out daily living skills with limited means, is as prevailing and effectual as any strategic planning Bill Gates or Michael Dell might use. While so many around us have the gall to complain about *not having enough,* for David and many others, success is defined by taking what is available and finding a way to make it work. Period. Dave van Cleave, it's you, baby!

It Came with the Job

Whether traumatically or congenitally, you must *qualify* for the great game of wheelchair basketball. Every participant meets some criteria through a loss, as the rite of passage is a paradoxical one.

I began my sports career in 1979, which placed me in the movement at a time when wheelchairs and wheelchair sports were evolving and the athletes and their training programs were infantile. Competitions grooved many avenues of expression but late night hotel room conversations were where the real friendships developed. As with the survivors of a shipwreck, our commonality nurtured our interaction. I was 20 years young when I began traveling on those trips and we spoke of intimate things during exploratory and emotional times. Impressed by each other's pathways, we all had a story.

A menagerie of disability and culture, the Dallas Raiders would load up in an old Parks and Recreation bus and head to Nashville or Lexington to strut our developing skill and the stuff *we thought* men were made of. And the trips home were always longer, which gave us time to lick our wounds and lie about what we would do the next time we faced the enemy. But hearing the war veterans candidly talk about another enemy held my fascination.

To hear Philip describe falling out of the gunner's window of a crashing helicopter, or Johnny talk about being sniped while walking point, or Joe describe the mysterious moment just before he stepped on a land mine, welded them to me. Every one of them held my intrigue but the following story I will always remember.

Lon was a Ranger who often went on reconnaissance missions. With specific instructions, he would be dropped, carry out a mission, then rendezvous with a helicopter at a certain location and point in time. If he wasn't there, the chopper would return without him and list him MIA.

After finishing a job once, he told us about waiting at the pick-up location, then seeing four Vietcong walk down the path towards him. Wincing during the narration, he said he hoped they would hurry on by or that the chopper would be late, but just as they were right on top of him, he heard the resonance of blades. I remember him telling me, "I didn't want to take them. If they had come just a little earlier, they'd have been by?" But hearing the approaching helicopter, unfortunately the four Vietcong squatted down right in front of him. It would either be him or them. In order to survive he knew what he had to do.

Jumping up just behind the enemy, Lon preserved his own life by taking theirs. The sound of the *hot area* caused the chopper to halt and hover, then with smoke Lon communicated that it was all clear. The Huey eventually came in as Lon stepped through the *new memory* and took refuge in the "bird."

It was the conflict between Lon's conscience and responsibility that struck a cord in me. Presented as if he was the manager of a store, dreading the fact that he would have to fire a poorly performing employee, he truly didn't want to engage the men, yet did what he had to do. These team members and the messages in their stories were as vivid as if I had been there and took me as close to war as I ever want to be. With total respect I tell this story.

Pushing Spirits and Pulling Wire

> *I've known successful sales people who were drunks, gamblers, liars and thieves...but I have never known a successful sales person who sat on his ass all day.*
> ✳ *Harvey Mackay*, Swim With the Sharks

My grandfathers were very special. We called my grandfather on my mother's side Big Gampie, a term handed down because at

141

an early age my mother couldn't pronounce the word grandfather. In addition he earned the title because he was 6'2" and weighed 250 pounds. But it was the way he lived his life that endeared us to refer to him as Big Gampie.

It was certainly risky in 1950 moving the family from New York to Las Vegas, but the opportunities to provide for his family tipped the scales so they pulled up stakes and headed for Nevada. As children my mom and her brothers, Buck and Don, would invade the house looking for heat relief, where Big Gampie would say "Get out of this house, people drive for hundreds of miles for the Las Vegas sun." Because of his hard work, Randy McElhone, from whom my surname comes, eventually earned ownership in the Nevada Beverage Company. The perks available and the people he knew in that business were *princely*.

He would move through Las Vegas wearing a huge white cowboy hat, managing his accounts and selling hundreds of cases of spirits, and as a promotion, would pass out bright green $2 checks torn from pads, which were given to cocktail waitresses and bar tenders as tips. At a party he once held for his clients, I remember sitting next to Johnny Weismueller, the Olympic champion and actor who played Tarzan. Another time, he rented a live tiger and placed it in a temporary cage in the front of the house as the guests were escorted to the property. He had a swimming pool in his backyard designed in the shape of a wine bottle with the baby pool serving as the cork. Once to promote a new scotch he was selling, he purchased a double-decker bus, had it shipped over from England and just for fun, drove us grandkids up and down the Las Vegas strip. Another time, the infamous "Bugsy" Malone had him tossed out of his office after he attempted to pick up payment for an order.

He made a genuine effort to intimately know his clients, writing down their names, kid's birthdays, special events, and any and all information available to him. He was there for them and he could sell. "AAAOOOHHH," Big Gampie was big!

My grandfather on my father's side was not as big in the physical form but demanded grandness from more of a subdued perspective. M.C. Snow, from whom my last name comes, was 5'9" tall, weighed 170 pounds, and to a four-year-old, warranted him the title of Little Gampie. He was not interested in presentation moreover he was big on being grounded in the simple yet significant things in life.

Growing up in Terrell, Texas, where Little Gampie lived, afforded us more time with him than Big Gampie. I have listened to Little Gampie tell stories of growing up in the Depression and having nothing to eat. He told me about the time his mother tied a string around the only piece of bacon she had. If one of the kids tried to swallow it, she would quickly remove it so the other kids would still have a chance to taste. Would kids be able to survive this today?

Little Gampie only completed the eighth grade but was a very successful electrician and worked as a fireman for 40 years. When I approached summer job age, my grandfather offered me employment working as an electrician's helper. This job presented a diversity of tasks, from replacing a simple wire in a house to crawling through the attic among bats and rats in 120-degree temperatures. I was amazed the first time I ever saw him prepare a house to be wired. We get these set images of people and when they venture out of how we normally see them, we must redraw the lines.

Pulling his old GMC pick-up truck to a house, my grandfather would get out five rolls of 12-gauge wire, pull out a huge drill and attack the naked framework. Deftly manhandling the drill, he could open every necessary pathway for the wire in about an hour. Once finished, we would break out the wire and start pulling it through each hole, tying it off at the electrical boxes. When you wired a house with my grandfather there was no messing around. I would help as much as I could but with sweat flowing down into his coveralls and a drop or two of blood on his callused hands, there was no question he was the point man. All of a sudden he would stop, pull out his handkerchief and say, "Let's go to lunch," and take me to the Dairy Queen for a Hungerbuster, fries and a Coke. On the way there, out of the corner of my eye I would glance over at him and relish in my pride.

On a plane once, I sat next to a lady named Laura who worked for Intel as a Planning Manager for Systems Manufacturing. Her primary responsibility was to hire and fire managers all over the world. I asked of her philosophy in how she treated employees once they were hired and she said, "The most important thing I do is treat them with respect, like I may work for them someday."

If you are willing to work, willing to do whatever it takes, in this world there is a place for you. My grandfathers knew how to work and how to treat people. Of all the things they taught me, the principle that I remember the most is that they suited up, showed up and gave it their best effort, whether afraid or not, and treated people right.

It's Not the Skill, It's the Will

> *All domains must contribute to winning but it is the emotional domain that affects performance the most.*
> ✳ *Sport psychologist Jim Loher*

I remember as a 10-year-old being mesmerized watching ants in an ant bed behind my house. Playing God, I stomped on the ant bed and disrupted their intricate network of pathways and responsibilities. To my *almighty* surprise, they received the "life blow," then incessantly began rebuilding the functional structure that had existed before. I'm not sure what I expected but in retrospect, what choice did they have? Not that ants hold secrets inaccessible to human beings, but the demonstration reminded me of how we must deal with adversity. We must *push forward*.

There are many big muscles in our bodies but none bigger than our heart. In commentary during the fifth set of the U.S. Open final on who might win between Andre Agassi and Todd Martin, John McEnroe said, "It isn't about talent at this point, it's about heart." The will of a person emulsifies success.

Continuous networking keeps a Paralympian abreast of the progress and performance of his competitors, but one never knows who will show up until they set wheel, cane or prosthetic device onto the field.

Cerebral Palsy sprinter Mario Duncan trained for four years to compete at the 1988 Paralympics in Seoul. With American talent so deep, surviving the national trials often presents an excellent chance at an international medal. Mario made the team as a short distance sprinter but upon arrival, was informed that not enough athletes qualified in his races so all of his events were canceled. Disappointed but patriotically steadfast, he stayed to support his fellow countrymen and enjoyed the best shopping in the world at Itawan. Since the window of opportunity at the Paralympic level isn't open very long, he quickly reaffirmed his decision to be the best in the world and vowed to win in 1992 in Barcelona.

Four years later Mario again survived the national trials and positioned himself as one of the favorites to medal. The U.S.A. team met in New York to brief—then boarded a plane for Barcelona. For your information, flying in a plane with 280 disabled athletes with different equipment and needs is like being in the bar in *Star Wars*. During the orientation, Mario was devastated as he again discovered that the minimum number of athletes had not been surpassed to qualify his category, which cancelled his events. As the tennis team leader, my responsibilities were to participate as a member of the U.S. Team Committee. We were devastated and sympathized. We all knew his story but there didn't seem to be any compensatory option. But later in discussions concerning who would carry the flag during the opening ceremonies, someone mentioned Mario.

There is great honor in carrying the flag during an Olympic or Paralympic competition. Athletes are selected not only for their athletic talent but also for what they stand for. Rafer Johnson, Muhammad Ali, Jesse Owens, all carried the flag for the United States with honor and dignity. Their stories are grand. For example in the 1936 Olympics in Germany, while the other countries dipped their flags in honor of the third Reich, in proud American fashion, Owens shocked the world by denying Adolph Hitler. This honor can establish the flag bearer as a national hero and the uniquely equivalent value of winning gold.

Agreeing that the acceptance of his fate represented what the American team was all about, our vote was unanimous. Mario was to bring the United States team into the opening ceremonies in front of 80,000 cheering Spaniards. I only regret not taking a picture of his face as we informed him of our decision. Mario never won a gold medal in Paralympic competition, but because of his will, a nation bestowed him an honor he and his descendants will be proud of forever.

In the final of the Japan Open, I had lost the first set 6–0 to Laurent Giamartini and was down 5–0 in the second. I couldn't seem to put together a combination that would produce games. The chagrin of losing a final that badly was so strong it didn't even bother me any more, I just wanted to win a few points. This attitude of wanting to win a point, of *putting myself into a position of winning a point,* actually distracted me from the embarrassment and I won a game. It was now 6–0, 5–1, so I decided to try it again, to focus on winning the next point. Winning the next game, I actually caused my opponent to become nervous, which allowed me to win the next two games, making the set score 5–4. I ended up winning the set in a tiebreaker and winning the third set 6–1.

No need in praising any mental toughness because it didn't exist, I was scared to death. The answer to this match and to life for that matter was demonstrated. I couldn't worry about the points I had lost as they were in the past. And I couldn't worry about the next points because they weren't there. But these two areas of the match were dominating my thinking to the point of self-destruction. When I focused on the present, I was able to make one of the greatest comebacks in all of wheelchair sports history. Even though we are afraid, sometimes we have to live life *one point at a time*.

Man's Best Friend

> *Lord please make me the person my dog thinks I am.*
> ✳ *Author unknown*

In *The Man Who Speaks To Horses* by Marty Robbins, I am reminded of the many lessons taught to us by animals concerning societal interaction and survival. Many similarities of social intercommunication, family dynamics and endurance are revealed while watching white-tail yearlings interact near a grove of mesquites, or a covey of bob white quail move in mobile trepidation, or a rock lizard fight for its life against a black racer snake. Referred to as the "harvest of truths" by author Steve Chapman, we can learn more from animals than we realize.

While fishing on the San Saba River near Menard, I kept hearing a "plop" in the water behind me. My curiosity eventually got the best of me as I was determined to figure out what was causing the sound. I let the river pull my kayak to the area of last "plop," where I found a floating half-gnawed green pecan. Upon further review, I noticed that all the pecans in the river were green and chewed.

Like an Apache, I stilled myself and watched for movement, then just behind a tree limb, the tail of an adolescent squirrel flickered. As I watched, I saw him scurry to a pecan, pull it from the branch and begin eating. Tricked by nature, he would disappointingly discard the immature nut letting it "plop" into the river, then locate another and repeat the process. The squirrel was very aggravated. In my own "harvest of truths" I was reminded of selfish moments in my life where I displayed similar immaturity and impatience. I usually want what I want, when I want it.

In an inverse comparison, the most unselfish animal on the planet is the dog. Early man domesticated dogs over 50,000 years ago. Being the better hunter of the two, Neanderthal would follow a hunting wolf pack. Once the pack's kill was made, man would chase the wolves away for the easy meal. Over time the abandoned wolf pups were taken in the hope of raising them to hunt for the clan. As man became more proficient at hunting, the wolf became more dependent on man. The "emotional similarities" forged a mutually beneficial bond. Creating their dependency, *we* have been "best friends" ever since.

Reminiscing their significantly healthy virtues, my offerings here are definitely Labrador-biased but most are cross canine transparent.

- If there is no place in heaven for dogs, I'm not going.

- Petting a dog should be a step in every 12-step program.

- Always thank a person for letting you pet their dog.

- Pet every dog you can. Demonstrate that you are not a threat by avoiding eye contact and approach them with a closed hand. Let them smell first, then give them your eyes, watch for the release, then you may approach. If a receptive sign isn't there, they are not comfortable. Don't let your ego get involved, respect their space.

- Upon entering a building and especially your home, go through the door first. It will confuse the pack instinct of your animal if you violate this.

- A dog would rather be with his owner and starve, than be alone and eat. As in following the instructions for the oxygen on an airplane, eat first then feed them.

- Dogs act like it, but they don't respect cats. Regarding who's better, have you ever heard of a cat saving its owner's life? That story in that book isn't true—don't believe it.

- Dogs don't discriminate against other dogs. An able-bodied dog will not act any different around a single amputee dog.

- Unlike the human personalities of the "workaholic" or "couch potato," dogs pace themselves for quality play and work.

- A dog will not hold onto an issue like a human being. They don't keep score.

- Thinking their owner is a culinary genius, a dog will eat everything on his plate.

- Figuratively speaking, unlike human beings, dogs *don't poop where they sleep.*

- Even to the dull and ignorant, they are the best listeners for they know there is a value in every voice.

- Dogs don't understand the meaning of words but are clear about the connection between sounds and emotions. They don't understand the phrase "bad dog" but rest assured they have no trouble sensing what you mean from your tone.

- Have you ever had your dog know that you are sad or that you have just made the decision to leave the house? They have the ability to feel your emotions and aren't *limited* by language. You can communicate with them without speaking. Think strongly of your dog and glance at him and see if he notices.

- They have incredible trust that things will always work out. This is sometimes confused with stupidity, but I assure you they are paragons of trust, faith, tolerance and patience.

- Their sense of smell is considered an emotion. Playing loud music to a sleeping dog will not arouse it, but bringing a hamburger into the room will awaken him immediately. We have lost this skill.

- Respect for wisdom in elders is a classic dog trait, which we are quickly forgetting.

- Wearing many hats, dogs serve as border patrollers, accomplices, comedians, flirts, co-pilots, taste-testers, huggers, athletes, heroes, and companions. They are also dishwashers, retrievers, pillows, wash clothes, napkins, alarm clocks, garbage disposals, hand warmers and blankets.

Eulogy to a Dog

Treat me kindly, my beloved friend, for no heart in the world is more grateful for kindness than mine. Do not break my spirit with a stick for though I might lick your hand between blows, your patience and understanding will more quickly teach me the things you would have me learn. Speak to me often for your voice is the world's sweetest sound, as you must know by the fierce wagging of my tail, when your footsteps fall upon my waiting ears. Please take me inside when it is cold and wet, for I am a domesticated animal, no longer accustomed to bitter elements. I ask no greater glory than the privilege of sitting at your feet. Feed me clean food that I may stay well to be ready, willing and able to protect your life, should it ever be in danger. And my friend, when I am very old and I no longer in good health, and I am not having any fun, do not make heroic efforts to keep me going. Please take my life gently. I shall leave this earth knowing with my last breath, my fate was always safe in your hands.

✳ *Author Unknown*

I have learned some beautiful lessons from our yellow lab Ginger, that in my opinion are worth ink. If you would like, replace her name with the name of your dog. I am sure it will fit just fine.

Ginger knows how to play hard yet knows the value and peace found in being still. While duck hunting once, she ran so hard, she couldn't even walk that night, but when my friend picked up his gun to clean it, without hesitation, she agonizingly stood at attention. She is appropriately quiet and reserved. Ginger, who honored her like an aristocrat, never disrespected Lady, our previous family canine.

After being scolded for eating a loaf of banana bread that was left on the countertop, Ginger took her punishment but didn't hold a grudge. She had let it go an hour later. While playing tennis, she would not take her eyes off me, even though the painful distraction of 200 tennis balls bounced all around her. Her loyalty was clearly demonstrated.

And around my nieces and nephews, her "pull-toy ability" is clearly displayed in her ultimate tolerance and love. Ginger is egoless, she doesn't care if she has the front seat or if anyone likes her, or if she has a nice house or good job. She loves being who and where she is. She just wants to go.

Pay It Forward

> *If you hold a light for someone else, you can't help but light the path for yourself.*
> ✳ *Battle of Independence hero and Texas Senator Deaf Smith*

In 1971 Rick Amber was flying combat missions over Vietnam. During his 109th sortie, anti-aircraft fire crippled his plane, which limited his chances of making it back alive. As his jet crashed onto the deck of the USS Hancock, he ejected and was catapulted into the control tower of the aircraft carrier. Rick crushed his shoulders and broke his neck, which paralyzed him from the fifth and sixth cervical vertebrae.

Medics were called while a serviceman immediately reached him to keep him from going into shock. Once stabilized, the medical team placed him on a helicopter to take him ashore. But due to inclement weather, the helicopter pilot experienced vertigo and crashed into the side of a mountain, killing and wounding several of the marines. Rick survived the crash and on a second helicopter, finally made it to the hospital.

Rick returned to the United States into the VA Hospital system less than enthusiastic and entered the rehabilitation process to learn how to live life as a quadriplegic. As my Uncle Joe would say about getting older, incurring a spinal cord injury in the 1960s was "not for sissies." The quality of rehabilitation was just evolving. But for the patient, there wasn't a choice; they had to do the work.

After years of mending, Rick went back to school and earned his Masters Degree in Environmental Science from the University of Dallas. It wasn't easy but he eventually became a teacher and a wheelchair tennis player, he married, and to the best of his ability, rejoined life. But in the center of his heart he was still a pilot and wanted to fly. Hand controls had evolved for disabled pilots with many taking to the skies, but what about for quads? Could he learn to fly again?

Placating himself with a teaching job, his extra time was devoted to the *possibility* of flying. Obvious hurdles included limited manual dexterity, transferring into the planes and finding the time and money that would allow him to pursue his dream. His persistence paid off as, not only did he attain his pilot's license, he eventually earned commercial accreditation as well. And the more he flew, the more he realized that many disabled people, and especially handicapped children, had not considered flying as a viable option.

Rick was always a *real dream* community developer. His contributions included starting a wheelchair basketball team, being an active member of a local wheelchair tennis club, appointment to the Dallas Area Rapid Transit Board and volunteering for many other community programs and boards. He loved helping people. His *dream* continued as he envisioned disabled pilots donating their time during "Fly Days," taking kids up in their airplanes. These events would not only be fun, but they would also display what people could do if they set their mind to it. The idea came to fruition in 1993 with the non-profit corporation called Challenge Air for Kids and Friends.

A few years later during a skydiving experience, Rick accidently fractured his leg. The medical check-up revealed "other complications" and Rick was diagnosed with bladder cancer. This isn't one of those miracle stories about a man's determination to beat the odds. Surrounded by family and endearing friends Rick elected to forgo a second round of chemotherapy and radiation and slowly succumbed to what author Terry Kay calls "the mutant cannibal."

The Dallas Morning News did an article about Challenge Air and the benefit to all the kids. It told Rick's story about the emergency landing on the Hancock, the act of the serviceman, the helicopter crash and his rehabilitation. After reading the story to her husband in a living room on the other side of Dallas, the wife of a Vietnam veteran asked, "Honey, weren't you on the Hancock?" Emotional, the retired serviceman walked over to his wife and said, "Yes that was my ship and I'm the serviceman they are talking about. He was immediately evacuated, I never knew his name." After 30 years, they reconnected, and on May 3, 1997, again held in the arms of this serviceman, Rick Amber "flew."

Today Challenge Air holds 25 national "Fly Days" a year and has offered thousands of kids the *real dream* of flying. Although Rick's life ended earlier than it should have, with his dream he *paid it forward*.

The national player of the year award at the U.S. Open Tennis Championships is named after Rick Amber and on September 19, 2000, I was presented with this prestigious honor. If only I had half of Rick's attitude! He understood kindness, the value of helping others and placed more weight on *giving* than on *taking*. By helping others, he became his dream.

For more information about Challenge Air see
www.challengeair.com

> *Many are at the shorefront waving goodbye as he sails over the horizon. But somewhere just beyond the horizon, there is another shoreline, with many on the beach saying, look, look, here he comes.*
> ✳ *Author unknown*

Chapter Fifteen

Stars

We all put our pants on one leg at a time.
✳ *Tom Snow*

Accountability

The most watched moment in sports isn't the Kentucky Derby or the kick-off of the Super Bowl; it's the lighting of the torch at an Olympic Games. There have been many great torch moments, but my favorite was in 1992 when Antonio Ribolo came out of the tunnel in Barcelona. I watched with intrigue because not only was there wonderment in what he might do with the bow in his hands, but he was limping.

Appropriately selected because he represented *both* competitions, Antonio was a Paralympic and Olympic archer from Spain. In front of the entire world, the flame courier lifted the torch as Antonio took an arrow from his quiver. Holding it up for the crowd and the world's approval, our attention was fixed as he lit the arrow, placed it in the string, pulled back and let it fly. The arrow expertly passed just above the cauldron and to the cheers of millions, the Olympic flame was lit.

So when the Atlanta Paralympic Organizing Committee contacted me to inquire if I would be interested in receiving the torch from President Clinton at the White House, without hesitation, I agreed. On the day my nephew Joseph was born, my once-in-a-lifetime experience began with an extensive security check and a briefing on the formalities of interacting with the President. Throughout the day I wasn't too anxious but when he walked around the corner into the Diplomatic Reception Room and reached out to shake my hand, for a moment I froze.

At that time President Clinton was running for his second term against Robert Dole, who in a desperate attempt to sway voters to his side had promised a 15% tax cut. I *advised* President Clinton not to worry because it seemed Senator Dole was "shooting threes." President Clinton looked at me and said, "Excuse me." I said, "President Clinton, when an opponent realizes the odds of winning a contest aren't good, desperate measures are taken. In basketball, we start shooting three point shots. Senator Dole is shooting threes." He said, "Oh, I see."

We were called to set up inside the door just before the ceremony was to begin. As the presidential band began to play, President Clinton poked me and said, "Come on, let's go." I knew we were supposed to wait until the band finished but since the President of the United States was prodding me to get a move on, I followed his direction. I figured if anybody could bail me out, the

President could. Once we were on the stage waiting for the formalities to end and the speeches to begin, President Clinton put his hand on my shoulder and said, "Boy I blew that. Sorry for sending you out early." I looked up at him and said, "No worries mate."

Writing about the President will probably invoke censorship. Nevertheless, the display of accountability deserves merit. When competing against athletes that blame, I will eventually win because I know they will find an excuse for things not going their way. By being accountable, we avoid victim mentality and the pitfall of blame, which arrests personal growth.

The time I spent at the White House will never be forgotten and especially the lesson from Bill Clinton in owning our mistakes.

※ *Thanks Marilyn!*

Humility

True self-esteem is thinking less about our self and more of our self.
※ *Coach Bill Hammett*

Paralympic athletes have the luxury of previewing the forthcoming excitement by watching the Olympics, which takes place three weeks prior. As I write here in South Carolina attending our last tennis tournament before Sydney, the opening ceremonies of the Olympics will be on television tonight. I will be in my room sponging up every minute.

I will never forget seeing an interview with the reserved yet mighty Yael Arad, the able-bodied judo athlete from Israel after she won a silver medal at the Olympics in Barcelona. Her interview defined humility. To that point in the history of the Olympic Games, no athlete had ever won a medal from Israel. Yael was the first.

Through open-ended questions, the reporter attempted to steer her into describing how special this feat was. Saucily, he said, "What you have done is unprecedented, you are the first, do you think they

155

will throw a party for you when you return to Tel Aviv?" Pausing briefly and in total humility, Yael said, "Well I don't know, I…I suppose so." I thought to myself, I suppose so? Are you kidding? To have won the first medal in the Olympics for any country would be large, but for patriotic Israel, it was huge! Surely she knows they will roll out the red carpet and embrace her with an all-out celebration. But I was refreshingly surprised and shocked with her response because even though the accomplishment was outstanding, her modesty and demureness kept her in check. Her attitude burned an indelible memory of humility in my mind.

Traveling in Israel three years later, with no real expectation, I asked if I might be lucky enough to meet her. "Of course you can, she lives over the hill." Shocked, I said, "She wouldn't mind?" "She is the daughter of Israel, her door is always open." Humility.

Either participating in front of thousands or just your family, wheelchair athletes never know how many people will attend an event. Promoted as the world #1, I had flown to Johannesburg, South Africa, to teach wheelchair tennis and after a 12-hour flight, we finally landed. As I deplaned I was shocked to see thousands of people in the lobby, 20 cameras, a procession of dignitaries, a performing Zulu tribe and fanfare everywhere. Unsure of what was happening, I assumed it was for me so I started waving.

Out of the corner of my ear, I heard a voice say, "It's not for you, over here mate, it's not for you." I looked around to see Craig, my friend from Petersburg, waving me over. As I arrived and reached out to shake his hand he said, "Look, mate." As I turned around, a group of athletes were coming off the plane led by Magic Johnson. Magic's All Stars had come to tour South Africa as well. Humility.

Another time I was on the United States wheelchair basketball team that had just arrived at Narita Airport in Tokyo. Here we were, the greatest wheelchair basketball team in the world, arriving to tour Japan and demonstrate our wheelchair skills. The Japanese international team, the media, newly injured with their therapists, and Japanese and American fans alike had filled the airport to officially welcome the best.

We entered the airport on a balcony that overlooked the baggage area, where everyone was waiting. There were elevators just down the hall, but right in front of us was an escalator, so we turned around to use the escalator and descend into the sea of supporters. The security attempted to stop us from boarding but we were Americans and were there to demonstrate our skill…and it would start right there. With 8 of us using the handrail for stability, it began to slip and as it slipped, we began to fall. This created a huge bottleneck of wheelchairs, artificial legs, backpacks, and cushions, along with several embarrassed members of the cocky U.S.A. team piled at the bottom of the escalator. Lacking confidence in the developing technology of escalators in Japan, we didn't attempt to ride any more moving stairs during that trip. Humility.

It is important for the experienced ones to share information. Shore feeding in the shoal areas of South Carolina is a learned behavior taught by dolphins to their young. They wouldn't know of this valuable feeding technique without the tutelage. Outings for the newly injured are similar as they provide a supervised practice environment with people *who have been there.*

The physical therapy department at St. David's Rehab had brought some of the patients out to the local wheelchair tennis tournament to see the top tennis players in the world. I was the fitness center coordinator at the time and believed it was important for these patients to not only witness high level tennis but to see that some of our local players ranked among the best.

There were 4 inpatients up against the fence of my court, watching me destroy this gentleman's unfortunate first round draw of playing the world #1. With the prowess of a professional, I reached back to hit a short ball and swung up as hard as I could. The shot was a winner but my follow through brought my racket right into my forehead, striking me just above the eye. The impact knifed my eyebrow, which immediately gushed blood. Dazed, I sat there applying pressure to my head and glanced over to see if any of the newly injured had noticed. Not only were they aware, they were already on their way back to the bus. Humility.

> *When you are being run out of town, stay just in front*
> *and make it look like it's a parade.*
> ✳ *Dub Gibbens*

157

The Key Is to Believe

The Dallas Youth Foundation gave me an award in 1986 for my accomplishments in Los Angeles. All night long they referred to me as a hero but the irony of the evening award was a *real hero* made the presentation.

Walter Payton was the headliner and I had the rewarding experience of spending time with him during the dinner. Affectionately referred to as "Sweetness," Walter was unpretentious, humble and inquiring. As the all-time leading rusher in the National Football League with over 16,000 yards, his accomplishments and attitude were exemplary. Similar to Earl Campbell, he ran the football as if it was just his occupation and not an *antithesis of insecurity*. Reminded of His plan, unfortunately at the age of 40, Walter Payton succumbed to liver cancer in 1999 and passed away.

During dinner that night we were involved in several small talk items, which surprisingly revealed his awareness and knowledge of wheelchair sports. He informed me that he saw the exhibition event that I was a part of in Los Angeles in 1984 and was impressed…and I was flattered. Having such a successful champion in my presence, I couldn't keep myself from asking about his philosophy of performance. What was he thinking when he attempted to escape players like Ronnie Lott or Lawrence Taylor? How did he prepare to perform? Where was he grounded that allowed him to run like no other?

As the conversation spun, Walter told me something I have never forgotten. He said, "Whether I am a better football player than the other man isn't important. If I convince myself to believe that I am better, something happens that takes priority over my physical ability. When I believe, it just happens. It's self-fulfilling." Empowering words from a powerful guy. What do you *believe*?

Hero

Whether valid or not, celebrity status lends credibility. Actors and sports stars can bring needed attention to all kinds of causes that would certainly be less known if not for their acknowledgment. The *paradox* has presented many opportunities for me to meet some of these stars and I am grateful to the many that have supported our movement. How many times have we assumed we knew a person, especially a public figure, then read about them or met them and found them completely different?

Before I met Christopher Reeve I disagreed with his "Cure Not Care" philosophy. This ideology suggested dollars be focused on finding a cure for people with spinal cord injuries, rather than be directed towards programs like counseling or recreation. Driven by the *exclusive assumption* of an unhappy life in a wheelchair, "Cure Not Care" assumed if dollars weren't being spent on research, they were being wasted. This partisan attitude disrespected the progress and milestones many of us had worked so hard to realize. I had spent the past 25 years of my life using my means to change societal perceptions. For someone to have only recently entered *the paradox* and label the life I fought so hard to forge as a miserable one, was not only erroneous but in my mind attacked my being.

While scientists worked on a cure, pursued their dreams, raised their families and padded their 401Ks, what were we supposed to do in the interim? Many others had spent a great deal of time positively affecting the world using their accomplishments and attitudes as advocacy, breaking down stereotypes, and in spite of the *horrible situation*, for the most part had created functional and rewarding lives. Were we to abandon the sacrifices, progress and newly developed means to a quality life? From wheelchairs and wheelchair sports, we were pursuing our dreams, raising our families and developing our 401Ks. It may sound absurd but why would we want a career change?

But there are severe inconveniences and frustrating struggles and *my perspective is from that of an active paraplegic and not from that of a person with a vent dependent cervical break*. And in their defense, fortunately most of the "Cure" campaigns have balanced their ideology, supported some welcomed contributions, and improved our quality of life. There have been many enriching additions like envitro fertilization, longevity studies and incontinence control that have come from their research. The older I get, the more I realize I don't know and concerning my perspective, I was wrong.

Who would have projected that Christopher Reeve would break his neck and champion our cause? As in the unfortunate situation of Magic Johnson acquiring the AIDS virus, did God place Mr. Reeve on our page? With respect to the sheer numbers and seriousness of spinal cord injuries and AIDS victims, it seems to me that the Divine Wind believed extra awareness here was necessary.

Risking controversy, I suspect a Higher intervention. Demanding attention, these two individuals, who unfortunately landed in their respective new worlds, could not have been hand picked any better. Who could have absorbed these predicaments or brought any more focus to these causes? I wouldn't wish a spinal cord injury or AIDS on anyone, yet who these individuals are, where they come from and how they have handled their situations is a godsend for the visibility needed to eradicate these problems.

After breaking his neck in 1980 in a football game playing for TCU against Bear Bryant's Crimson Tide, Kent Waldrep founded the National Paralysis Foundation and immediately started raising money for research. Invited by Kent, Christopher Reeve was to speak at an upcoming NPF Gala. Kristi Thomas, President of Accessology, asked us at Allumed to provide Mr. Reeve's medical equipment during his stay. Securing an extensive list that included two large vans with lifts, we waited for his plane to arrive in the JC Penney hangar at Love Field. Being the public figure that Reeve was, forced us to incorporate very strict security measures. Once the plane pulled into the hangar and the doors were closed, we unloaded the luggage, then transported his entourage of six full-time staff members to the Anatole Hotel.

In his speech he publicly asked for needed funds, then stated without the money, spinal cord research wouldn't be able to secure the best scientists. As a recent example, AIDS research had had the support of vast resources, which helped secure some of the most brilliant minds. This resulted in a *resolution* of the problem as living with AIDS today is a manageable situation. Secondly, he spoke about his desire to walk, but acknowledging reality, said he at least hoped for improvement. "If I could just breathe on my own and get function in one hand, imagine how much my life would be improved." He continued by promising that scientists would not stop until they found a cure for paralysis. The third point he enlightened us to was, the progress that was being made wasn't isolated to spinal cord research but spilled over to all neurological disorders like Hodgkins, Muscular Dystrophy, Multiple Sclerosis and Parkinsons; they are all related. As I mentioned earlier, initially I wasn't a fan, but after hearing him speak, publicly and personally, Christopher Reeve won me over.

Working out in the fitness gym the next morning, his program manager said, "Do you think he really needs to do this, do you think he needs the money? He could be writing and directing movies, and spending time with his kids. He is so tired, yet he understands his responsibility and will continue this fight because it is the right thing to do."

Before leaving, Reeve generously allowed us a photo opportunity and as people scurried to get their cameras, for a few moments we were left alone. Two completely different people living two completely different lives that probably never would have crossed if it had not been for our accidents, we were connected by circumstance.

I said "Mr. Reeve, I disagreed with the research movement for a long time but after spending time with you, I have become a fan. I am sorry this has happened but you have divinely come to us with strength and action." Initiating his respirator to fill his lungs, he looked at me, winked and said, "Stick with me, we will get this done together." Definite Hero!

The Highest Form of Flattery

Impersonation is a compliment to the impersonated.
❋ *World Team Cup coach Byron Trapp*

Steve Welch and I were asked by consummate wheelchair tennis supporter Tina Dale and the USTA Florida Section to participate in a wheelchair tennis exhibition at the Nuveen Masters Tennis Tournament in Naples, Florida. What an honor to have the opportunity to display our skills at such a posh event as John McEnroe, Mats Wilander, Jimmy Conners and Bjorn Borg headlined the all-star cast. Having severely belittled several fans and linesmen, McEnroe won the match but wasn't the crowd favorite and ended the match being the "goat" of the evening.

Mac and Wilander exited the court after finishing their three set match, then Welch and I entered to an enthused crowd of 7,000, and began warming up for our singles exhibition. I had turned away to get a few balls from the ball boy and when I looked back, John McEnroe was on the other side of the court holding his tennis racket and talking with Steve. All of a sudden Steve began pushing away from Mac towards my side of the court. As I looked back over the net, John pulled his racket back and said "Are you ready?" I didn't know what to say. In shock I think I just nodded my head up and down. I certainly wasn't going to pass up the opportunity to hit tennis balls with this legend.

What initially began as a ground stroke rally quickly evolved into playing points with one of the greatest players of the game. Realizing this all time dream initially made Steve and me nervous but in time we began to settle in. During one of the points I had been pulled to the net where I directed a volley towards the sideline for a winner. After John called the ball out, I threw my racket down in McEnroe form and yelled, "You can't be serious!"

After a brief moment of deduction, the crowd realized the *psyche* and came in with laughter and delight. Grinning, Mac prepared to hit another serve and humorously said, "Now that's what I like to see." In an instant, flattery had not only bridged our lives but the crowd had also connected in this spontaneous tennis spectacle. And no longer was Mac the "goat."

Mirroring has its advantages and "buddying" with the handicapped guys carries a little weight as well.

Faith without Works is Dead

Personally, I don't want any help...unless it's not offered. But offering it without checking with me takes away my choices and sometimes awakens a sleeping lion. I know it's hard to believe, but even I have used my chair to gain an advantage.

There is a certain amount of manipulative power inherent in a disability. To some, a wheelchair is like capital, just waiting to be converted into profit. And there exist many types of profit like a discounted price or good seat at a concert or cutting a long line at Six Flags. Some call it resourceful, others manipulation—there exists a fine moral line as to the definition of a win. An exceptional win is to get bumped up to first class on an airline, especially on an international flight. Whether this happens because of practicality or pity, I have never known a handicapped person, or anyone for that matter, to turn down a first class seat.

I was at Chicago O'Hare Airport attempting to board a flight to Dallas. My connection was late which pushed my boarding to last, rather than the usual first. I would now have to transfer to the isle chair and be ushered down the compact passageway of gawking people. Having been on the road for awhile, this put me in a "snitty" mood. If I am in a healthy state, I usually employ tolerance, but if I am tolerantly bankrupt, I stay a "snit." And on this particular flight I was being a "real snit."

Realizing my inconvenience and aggravation, the Customer Service agent temporarily "de-snitted" me by bumping me to first class, which allowed me to wheel onto the plane and easily transfer into my seat. Removed of my steerage mentality, I quickly made the transformation to bourgeoisie.

An article in *Forbes Magazine* said, "First class is a great place to meet people and make contacts, as one never knows whom they will meet." Maybe so, but after hearing that I compete in wheelchair sports, sometimes people want to head into that "you really are amazing" garbage, so I usually shun any initial body language that might invite dialogue. I couldn't deny, though, that on that day, the lady next to me was different. Something pulled me into talking to her and we introduced ourselves. "Hello, my name is Ann." "My name is Randy." Since the early part of the flight was extremely bumpy, prayer coincidentally became the topic.

As we began to discuss God, we visited what we thought He was, how He was involved in people's lives and why some were more comfortable than others with their relationship. I made the comment that I thought a spiritual relationship was very important and that finding God was vital, yet sometimes I hadn't a clue as to what finding Him meant. There was so much struggle and strife in the world, and so many questions. Most of the time I ended up confused. I informed her that I pray all the time.

Calmly Ann said, "Finding God is not as important as *seeking* God. Religion attempts to interpret Him, yet God is individual and is inside us all. The *continuing work* toward a perfect relationship with Him, which never really exists, is our job description. Meditate more so he can speak to you. The *seeking* is the key."

As she gathered her things and disappeared into Dallas, one of the flight attendants said, "Wow, you were in such a long conversation with her, what did she say?" "Re-snitting" myself, I ignored her question and asked about my wheelchair, wondering what her excitement was all about. Then she said, "Isn't she wonderful?" "Who?" "Ann Landers."

Father, Thou knowest I am growing older.
Keep me from becoming talkative and possessed with
the idea that I must express myself on every subject.
Release me from the craving that I must
straighten out everyone's affairs.
Keep my mind free from the recital of endless detail.
Seal my lips when I am inclined to
tell of my aches and pains.
Teach me the glorious lesson that occasionally
I may be wrong.
Make me thoughtful but not moody,
helpful but not bossy.
With my vast store of wisdom and experience
it seems a pity to not use it all,
but Thou knowest, Lord, that I want to keep
my friends until the end. Amen.
✳ *Author unknown.*

Chapter Sixteen

Laughter

A touch of madness will help you get through the day.
✳ *Paralympian Bruce Karr*

Seat Belts

Early in our new bodies, we attempt to avoid embarrassment; this is the last thing a person in a wheelchair wants. Risk taking is seized slowly with attempts just outside the comfort zone. Examples might be wheeling a long distance, pushing up a semi-steep ramp, or even going to a bathroom in an unfamiliar restaurant. Later, sophomore risks are attempted like a public transfer out of the chair. This may include a bathtub or down to the ground, or even up on a counter to reach a plate. Finally as a veteran, we may endeavor into the back seat of a car, on to a riding lawn mower or maybe even into a boat. But a ride at the fair is considered a *master transfer*.

The Zipper is one of the most popular rides ever. Within the safe environment of a cage, the body mass of an able-bodied participant is supported by functioning muscle. For a disabled rider, though, the situation demands a little more respect. So when the employee working the Zipper asked if I was sure I wanted to ride, I should have remembered rule #69–Section 3.1Ab77 from the "Handbook for Gimps" about public humility and seriously considered my decision. But I offered him the same answer I told the Eiffel Tower employee when I wanted to go the final three flights of stairs, which is the same thing I tell rental car agencies when I want to rent a car without having to pay for hand controls (I use a tennis racket). I just say, "Sure, I can walk." Of course I never tell them about the time our wheelchair basketball team was driven by two double amputees, with one of them operating the steering wheel and the other on the floor managing the brake and accelerator. Hey, the gym was only a couple of miles away.

As the ride employee held the door, I positioned my wheelchair next to the cage, which provided a stable transfer point into the contoured seat. Once there, I held myself in as Kuerzi locked the padded support beam across our bodies. Although the people waiting in line would have disagreed, I was fine.

The first indication that things weren't going well was when the worker moved our car to a different height to let others into their cars. I immediately slipped and wedged into the corner of the beam like a leaf under a windshield wiper. My trusty denial arrived and spoke loudly as I still *believed* I would be OK. But as we began to "zip", centrifugal force pulled me from under the beam and slung me into the bottom of the ride. Immediately my friend pushed down with his legs and stuffed me into the corner. This was not a good situation. As we went by the control area, we yelled, "Stop, Stop, Stop...HEEEEEELP"...but our pleas were incognito because everyone was yelling that.

Flopping a few more times, the ride employee finally realized I was separated from my seat and ended our ordeal. As the ride stopped, I settled to the bottom of the cage and when he opened the door, like pancake batter, I poured out onto the ground. It was the people who had arrived after I transferred into the ride that were really confused.

After convincing everyone I was OK, I asked for my chair, transferred in, brushed myself off and went out into the State Fair. A bit further down the Midway, Kuerzi looked at me as we approached the "Black Widow." We quickly canceled eye contact and steered towards the sanctuary of the cotton candy booth.

It Isn't What It Seems

Until we actually spend time in someone else's shoes, we cannot testify as to what quality of life they really have. In 1996, the National Spinal Cord Injury Association reported that only a small percentage of the general public felt that quality life in a wheelchair was possible, yet most people in wheelchairs felt their life was a quality one. Companies frequently substitute job tasks to ensure employee sensitivity. Whatever the case, the benefit of the *first impression*, which is intended to shortcut its user in understanding a person, more often than not creates misunderstanding.

I have written about subtle discriminations and cognitive distortions that may seem trivial to the general population, but to a wheelchair user, these are blatant and rude. Before you employ a first impression, I challenge you to one hour of wheelchair mobility in a mall. You will know what I mean.

For an able-bodied coach, the best way to learn about the minutiae of wheelchair tennis is to spend time in a chair. Ever since their first experience, Bal and Marcha Moore had been committed to wheelchair tennis, directing camps, teaching lessons and coaching on international teams. Yet early in their careers, they felt they were lacking in the finer points of teaching the sport. They spent time in some of the athlete's chairs during events, but still hadn't had a real opportunity to refine their skill.

After inquiring, Quickie Designs, the champion in manufacturing sports and everyday wheelchairs, donated products to the Moores for chair skill development. Excited about returning to their summer home in Rhinelander, Wisconsin, where they had not been in months, they immediately took out their new toys, "saddled up" and began playing wheelchair tennis.

Looking like rookies, each began maneuvering their chair around the court. Even though they were making laymen mistakes, they were learning about the importance of movement blended with stroke execution. Acknowledging the feeling that they were being watched, they simultaneously stopped their practice and looked towards the fence to see their neighbors who were standing there speechless. Since they hadn't seen their friends all summer, Bal said, "Hey there, how's it going." Mr. Carroll said, "Oh my God, Bal, what has happened?" Not realizing anything was wrong, Bal and Marcha just looked at each other. At that moment Judy Carroll said, "When did it happen?" Suddenly, the Moores realized that the Carrolls had no idea they weren't permanently disabled. Sports wheelchairs fit tightly so when Bal tried to get up, he stumbled out of the chair. Struggling, he said, "Wait, let me explain." Mr. Carroll yelled out, "No, stay there." Adding to the Carroll's shock, Bal and Marcha then stood up out of their wheelchairs and began walking towards the fence.

Once explained, it was finally clear, yet the Carrolls still had a hard time understanding why anyone would want to be in a wheelchair if they didn't have to.

Combat Conditions

As in having children, changing jobs or a difficult transfer, unless we venture, we will never know. For a disabled individual, venturing into overseas travel can provide valuable lessons and learning moments, and of course some great stories.

Once again, I apologize to the French, but hey, "c'est la vie." Talk about egos, just like Texans, they have a huge one. In my opinion, France is one of the most "gimp unfriendly" places in the world, not only from a physical perspective but from an attitudinal one as well. We just don't matter. Regardless, Paris offers much in culture with its history, museums, architecture and cuisine. Certainly the Louvre is a tourist favorite but I enjoy the impressionist paintings in the Musee d' Orsay. Always is a powerful word, but we *always* went into Paris during our sports trips, if for nothing else than to devour a chocolate crepe under the Eiffel Tower.

During orientation at the World Track Championships, Coach Judy Einbinder acknowledged the abundant free time, but sternly reminded us of our racing priorities. Any athlete could travel into Paris but missing the midnight curfew meant automatic removal from the team and immediate deportation back to the States. As overall team leader, Judy was also our personal coach, which carried supplementary responsibilities, pressures and penalties. To cross her would be *muy malo* as there would be no deferred adjudication.

With our races later in the week, Robert, Bill and I decided we better "do Paris" early so we sought out the closest train station, which was Ecole' Centrale and embarked on the twenty-five minute ride. Time seemed to fly as we stopped at all the tourist spots. We ascended to the top of the Eiffel, rode the Prada, cruised the Champs Elysses, toured Notre Dame, and it was at Harry's New York Bar where we realized it was 10:55 p.m.

Like leaving a burning building, we were out of Harry's to find the nearest train station. After interpreting the schedules and finding our track, we finally heard our train approaching but lost our breath as we realized *it was on the wrong side of the track.* Train schedules can be very confusing, especially if everything is communicated in a foreign language. Knowing that our *lives* depended on being on that train, the only way to board was to scoot up a flight of stairs, cross a bridge, and bump down a similar stairway on the other side.

In a panic we transferred out of our chairs, and began scooting, pulling up one step at a time. Without any help from the passing French pedestrians, we finally arrived at the top of the platform, hopped into our chairs, traversed the bridge, and began descending the opposite side. We breathed a sigh of relief as we wheeled into the very first car. Robert mentioned that we were very fortunate to have made the train to Ecole' Centrale. In broken English the purser informed us that the train we were on was not going to Ecole', but to Orly. With our frozen attention, he turned and pointed out the window at a train that had just pulled up at the platform from where we had just come, and said, "Train, Ecole' Centrale." It was 11:25 p.m.

Just beating the closing doors, we bolted out of the car to backtrack our recent achievement. As we bounced down the last few stairs, the doors of our train closed and it slowly pulled away. We were doomed; it was 11:35. Pondering how we would explain to our sponsors and the National Wheelchair Athletic Association why we were back in America so early, we noticed a taxi parked just below the station. The taxi driver was truly startled as three wheelchair athletes sprinted towards and invaded upon his cab. With our chairs stuffed everywhere, we attempted to communicate our destination, then finally yelled, "Ecole' Centrale," and with the newly found ability to interpret English, the driver sped off. The fare for a 20-minute cab ride was $56 American.

Enjoying a late-night cup of coffee in the cafeteria, Judy was rewarded with the arrival of *her children* as we headed off for bed at 11:59.

With most emergencies, and especially gimp train travel in France, sometimes *combat conditions* are necessary to survive.

Out "of" a Limb

Norm lost his leg in a nasty motorcycle crash when a lady pulled out in front of him, causing him to lay down his bike. In the hope of avoiding a major injury, his strategy was correct but futile.

Amputees are the envied ones in the disabled world because physical and biological function is minimally affected. But even though they are less affected functionally, they draw more attention from the able-bodied population due to the visual shock value of missing a limb or three. Whether accepted or not, many spinal cord injuries wish their only concerns were to be missing a limb. Simply put, we wish we were amps. In fact we wish we were amps with big fat settlements. That would be *gimp nirvana*. Amp envy reminds me of what we would sing when racers like Jim Martinson would kick our butts in sports, "ode to be, a double amputee."

Norm was an aspiring fisherman. He had borrowed some equipment from a friend and had headed to the Guadelupe River to catch anything that swam his way. After casting several times, one of the expensive lures came loose from the line and began floating down the river. Luckily, it caught on a limb under a tree that was lying in the water. Hobbling through the woods, Norm climbed up into a tree then out on a limb, and attempted to retrieve the lure. As he leaned over, the suction that held his prosthesis to his stump gave way, and his limb slipped through the legging of his shorts and plunked into the river below.

Notwithstanding the cost, which sometimes can reach $15,000, the function of his limb was very important, especially during the mobility challenge of a fishing trip in the woods. Norm was now *paralyzed* as his limb bobbed in the current heading towards the Weberville dam.

As it was about to disappear, Norm noticed that his limb caught on another limb that was projecting from the shore. Carrying the fishing pole, which in no way would function as a limb, Norm hopped on his good limb through the woods to a prime casting spot and began casting in hopes of recovering his limb from the limb. He persistently cast several times and finally hooked his limb from the limb, reeled it back and replaced it next to his good limb. Norm then gathered the equipment and headed to his vehicle using both limbs vowing never to be out *on*, or out *of*, a limb again.

If We Couldn't Laugh We'd All Go Insane

Laughter is the welcomed and undeniable first step towards acceptance. A person is on their way when they can chuckle in the face of calamity.
✳ *Wendy Gumbert, coach of the gold medal quad rugby team in Sydney*

Society tells us it's inappropriate to laugh at a person who is *supposedly* less fortunate than us. But if this restriction can be removed, not only can the laughter be a surprise, it can also be very enjoyable. Like being in church with the giggles, the forbidden nature of the laughter makes it even funnier.

Let's try it. People with cerebral palsy control their extremities with varying degrees of difficulty. With the milder cases, some of them are able to ambulate. Relaxing and controlling their spasms is key. Imagine a kid with cerebral palsy coming out of a swimming pool and stepping onto very hot concrete. As the sizzling concrete over-stimulates his spasms, his entire synchronicity is tweaked and in an awkward sort of dance, he stumbles towards the relief of the grass, slurring, "Ouocsh, ouoosscsh, uocsh." I thought it was pretty funny myself. The following are a few forbidden nature stories that might just tickle the giggle box. As with crying, once the decision is made, it flows. If you are offended, I apologize, but I'm sure you will get over it.

We took a group of disabled kids to Six Flags for a day of fun. Taking someone in a wheelchair to Six Flags is highly encouraged because we get great parking, don't have to wait in line and are allowed two turns on the rides. *I just hate being in a wheelchair.*

After being escorted past the queue of waiting riders, we transferred onto the ground next to the roller coaster and our chairs were removed. When the disabled get out of their wheelchairs onto the ground, it makes people very uncomfortable. And for the riders in the car that pulled up after we had transferred, it was even more confusing. Why twelve people were sitting on the ground next to the ride was definitely an enigma.

With a very diverse group of gimps, once the car emptied, we began transferring into our seats. Off we went, flying around corners, up and down, with centrifugal force affecting our paralyzed parts like coins in a dryer. All of a sudden, about halfway through the ride, I heard 16-year old Trey behind me yelling "Oh, Oh, OOOOOhhhhh Noooooo!" I feared for the worst. With his hand over his face as we pulled up to the platform, Trey said, "My eye, my eye, my eye is gone." Trey's glass eye had been sucked out of its socket and was nowhere to be found.

As the waiting able-bodied riders attained a new level of discomfort, the ride temporarily shut down and all the employees scoured the grassy area below for Trey's glass eye. Just as everything was settling down, one of the staff shouted, "Here it is." Using a napkin from his pocket, he picked up the eye, ascended the steps and handed it to Trey. The waiting riders watched in shock. While sitting in the seat of the roller coaster, Trey wiped it off, spit on it and slipped it back into the socket. As he looked up at the staff member he said, "Thanks, dude."

After transferring back into our chairs, I considered offering a supportive debriefing, but as I looked back at the crowd, I decided they had had enough.

Even though all disabled have common ground, our injuries, disciplines and idiosyncrasies are specifically unique. I consider myself very sensitive but often my naiveté is exposed. While driving with my friend Pat, the Executive Director of the Texas Governors

Committee for Disabled Persons, I must have inserted my foot into my mouth a hundred times. By the way, don't use the cliché, "put your foot in your mouth" around a double amputee. It can be embarrassing once you remember they don't have any feet.

Pat, who is completely blind, opened my eyes (pun intended) to many things during our trip from Laredo to Austin, but the cutest was a slang term specific to her segment of the disabled world. As people in wheelchairs use the term gimp, the blind affectionately refer to each other as blinks. Don't ya' love it? Hey blink, WAASSSSSSUUPPPP! Crossing cultural lines can be dangerous though, and sometimes invoke anger or outcast. I would feel very uncomfortable calling someone a "blink," yet because I am a member of the wheelchair community, I freely use the word "gimp." Safely used within a culture, a slang term identifies you as part of the group.

During the drive, I must have seemed insensitive because I felt like I used every sight cliché in the book. "Look at that, what did he look like, what color was it, look over there, can you see my point"…I *saw* no end. She later said it was cute how I stumbled through our conversation. Never seeing it before, to hear her describe the color green as temperate was intriguing. Spending time with her was very enlightening and if you ever get the chance to meet her, don't forget to ask about the time she *fell into the manhole*.

At the Paralympics in Atlanta, I was with a couple of the U.S. basketball team members when a partially blind runner came jogging by. As he approached he began clearing his throat, and sent a "lung biscuit" just over our heads. In shock we simultaneously ducked and yelled. As he turned his head back towards us he said, "Sorry, I didn't know you were there."

Another time, Craig and I were traveling on a bus to our dormitory after watching the U.S. women win another basketball game. They were awesome and I was so proud because the best player, Ruth Nunez, came from our program at St. David's Rehabilitation Center in Austin. To quote John Galland, a paraplegic from a snow skiing accident, "None of us got a paraplegic manual when we came home. There is nothing quite like the words of someone who has already been there to help you along." Mike Haynes did a super job with Ruth.

Craig and I noticed some cute girls dozing just across from us. Rather than simply saying, "Hello, how are you, where are you

173

from, want to get a coffee?" or offering something seamless like, "Did it hurt?"… "What?"… "Falling from the stars?"… or something really smart like, "You are the reason cavemen chiseled on caves," we opted to flirt with them using a more advanced strategy.

As the bus driver hit the brakes, as loud as we could we both screamed, "AAAAAAHHHH!" as if our bus was about to be in an accident. It worked great, but what we didn't realize was the blind Belgian swim team was also on the bus. Looking like *normal* people, we had no idea they couldn't see. Every person on the bus screamed and leaped up into the air to save their life.

Well, not only did we ruin the possibility of meeting the girls, who didn't think our stunt was advanced at all, we wrecked any and all relations between the United States and blind sports associations in Belgium.

Fishing guru Shorty Powers had taken a break from his PVA Bass Trail Tour and had driven to Kansas City for the National Disabled Bowling Tournament. Being a legend, he arrived fashionably late for the start and wheeled into the huge bowling alley that entertained 200 disabled bowlers. As he carried his bowling ball in his lap and greeted everyone, he was distracted from the fact that every other pathway down to the alleys had two steps. Caught up in salutations, he committed himself to a wrong entryway and plunged headfirst down the steps. *Gravity and the disabled have a love-hate relationship.*

Airlines can be hard on wheelchairs. Judging from the condition our rides are sometimes returned, one would tend to believe that a group of gorillas carry out baggage-handling responsibilities. To protect our chairs, we sometimes store them in travel crates that have roller wheels. Packing a delicate 15-lb. racing chair insulates it from the potential in-transit abuse. Athletes will frequently attach these travel cases to their everyday chairs using a rope or chain, and aspiring to be as independent as possible, will pull them through airports and hotels.

Gary had just arrived in Atlanta to participate in the Peachtree Road Race. The nationally recognized 10-Kilometer Championship offered a record-setting course with accommodating amenities and supportive personnel. He checked into the Hyatt, planned to go to his room, unpack his things and relax. As the elevator doors opened, he backed the crate in first, then himself. Just as the doors were about to close, a gorgeous lady walked up, decided she couldn't fit in the elevator and said, "It's OK, I'll wait." Beauty sometimes anaesthetizes lucidity. Forgetting he was attached to his travel case, Gary quickly pushed out of the elevator to say hello, and just missed the closing elevator doors. As he began speaking, the elevator with the crate still inside, began to ascend. Suddenly his wheelchair was jerked out from under him and pulled to the roof, which flipped Gary out on the floor. As he looked up at the girl, the rope snapped and his chair crashed down on top of him, and broke his collarbone. There is nothing like a great first impression.

Wheelchair life affords perfect opportunities for shock humor. As long as it's not at the expense of another, humor is healthy. Doing something to freeze an innocent bystander is rewarding but nothing I have ever done could accomplish the enjoyment of the following.

Joe was avant-garde, a generation X'er. He changed the color and style of his hair frequently, and his clothing was statement-based. Once I saw him complete the entire Tulsa Run, which was held during Halloween, wearing a monster mask. His attitude was always young.

Joe's birth defect left him without any legs. He had used a skateboard for a mobility base since he was a kid. Sitting on his skateboard, he would reach forward with his hands, then quickly push in a posterior direction and cruise his house, neighborhood and school. The result of this style of mobility had perfectly molded his upper body for wheelchair sports so when he found wheelchair racing, he had an advantage.

We were competing in Eugene, Oregon, in the Prefontaine Classic 10-K Race, and after finishing a training session, had stopped to get a drink at a fast food drive-through. Deciding the young female employee was taking way too long, Joe reached from the seat of his Volkswagen bus and opened the drive-through window. He then jumped up on the windowsill, transferred into the store, scooted along the counter, pulled out a cup and began pouring his own drink. Here was a huge double amputee with orange hair sitting on the counter of a fast food restaurant in clear view of the inside customers, serving himself. The look on her face as she rounded the corner was priceless.

Another story involved a man from Michigan named Craig, who had lost his legs in an industrial accident. He had fallen into a metal crushing device, which quickly made mush of his lower appendages. The accident didn't stop him from living though, because he became successful in sales, athletics and fatherhood. With most of the team traveling from outside of California including myself, Wayne had built our national-caliber basketball team around Craig. To win in those days, people had to be flown in. Wayne said, "I didn't start this mess but I'll be damned if it's going to beat me."

On one of our flights, we had pre-boarded the plane and were waiting for the able-bodied passengers when Craig opened the overhead storage and swinging like a monkey, leaped in. Before he closed the door, he told us to ask a flight attendant for a blanket, and to point to the storage unit where he was hiding. In a few moments, a male flight attendant happened down the aisle so we eagerly carried out his instructions. When the unsuspecting flight attendant opened the door, Craig dropped out and grunted. The flight attendant was so surprised he screamed and actually fell back on one of the other players.

> *Just as removing ice from the wings of an airplane,*
> *laughter thaws away the pain, allowing us to freely fly.*
> ✳ *Kristi Thomas*

Commit First and Figure It Out as You Go

My family grew up on Lake Tawakoni, a reservoir near Dallas where we frequently enjoyed fishing, water skiing and tubing. I had been home from rehabilitation about six months and couldn't wait to go to the lake with my friends. I hadn't figured out the logistics of using the bathroom yet, but I didn't care, I was going to the lake.

Slightly self-conscious, it was my first time back in a boat. But being with a couple of good friends and their girl friends helped me relax. After being on the water for several hours, I couldn't put it off any longer; I had to pee. Devising a diversionary plan of *false swimming*, I prepared to enter the water, but as I scooted to the edge, my pants snagged a boat cleat, which was bolted to the top of the boat. As I carried out a *controlled fall* into the water, the boat cleat held my pants and hung me over the side like a stringer of fish. With my head level with the water, I yelled, "Oh...HELP, HELP!" One of my friends jumped up and freed me by ripping my pants away from the cleat. As everyone stood, I flopped into the water.

To help reduce the immediate embarrassment, my friend said, "Hey, Randy, do you think you can ride the inner-tube?" I told them I could but wondered, what would happen to me while on the tube? Could I hold on? What would happen to my legs? After a bit of a struggle, I climbed on top and off we went. It wasn't too hard holding on, and initially everything went fine. All that strength training in physical therapy had really paid off. But then things began to go wrong as I felt like I was being pulled from behind, but I held on like a baby opossum under its mother. Wondering why my friends were staring at me, I looked back over my shoulder. Surprisingly, I saw my feet skipping off the water like seat belts that were hanging through the closed door of a moving car. From the shore I must have looked like a giant fishing lure. Traumatized, I let go of the inner tube and splashed into the water. But I wasn't about to give up.

As the boat pulled up, my friends asked if I was OK. I said, "Yes I'm fine. I want to go again." Surprised, my friend said, "OK...but don't forget to wave at everybody on the beach, they want to see you riding." With my butt down this time, I felt very stable and much more secure. They increased the speed and it felt great to ride again. The nostalgic moment was fleeting though, because just as we pulled by the beach, the water rushing under the inner tube grabbed my soaked, stretched and ripped sweat pants and pulled them down to my knees. I don't think that's what my friend meant when he said "wave to everybody."

Commit first and figure it out as you go.
✴ *Alison Norton*

Outside the Box

Once I was sitting in the cafeteria with my friend Beth, a Recreational Therapist at Baylor Institute for Rehab when all of a sudden a man burst into the crowded cafeteria being chased by another man firing a 25-caliber pistol. This happened within a few feet of where we were sitting. With the entire cafeteria in shock and all of us ducking our heads, we later discovered the pursued man hid in a closet in the emergency room. Once the scene was under control, this stroke of luck actually expedited emergency surgery, which saved his life. Life is uncertain. When bad things happen, we wonder about God's will, yet sometimes forget we are His and don't have the right to His will. Our job is to keep it simple, do our best, help others, and let Him do the rest.

A drunk driver made some new acquaintances one day by crashing head on into oncoming traffic. Jackie was killed and Shorty died on the operating table three times before surviving as a paraplegic. The impact of the crash ripped Shorty's aorta from his heart, which deprived his spinal cord of oxygen. Since he lived for the outdoors, one might assume that his options might now be limited, but not Shorty. Elaborating about options after his injury, John Galland said, "Before my skiing accident I could do 10,000 things. Now I can do about 7,000. Focusing on the 3,000 things I can no longer do will make me miserable."

Shorty and John were pioneers of backwoods recreation in the '70s. To venture into the woods in wheelchairs and pursue waterways with kayaks was unheard of, but for these guys, missing out was not an option. Pushing their limits, they craved the challenge. They called themselves two gimps, two wheelchairs, two kayaks and a four- wheel drive...looking for water.

My first real *outside the box* challenge was not wheelchair basketball or wheelchair tennis. Those programs were safe for me because I could easily retreat if an *accident* occurred. My first real adventure was a three-day river trip that Turning POINT had organized exclusively for the disabled. Shorty called me in 1979 and informed me to meet him just below the Mansfield Dam near Waco. The morning I left Austin, I thought, "How were we going to get the kayaks down from the trailer, set up campsites, and deal with personal hygiene issues for three days? How will we manage without any help?"

Sparing your time and paper, it turned out to be one of the most rewarding "personal growth" experiences I have ever completed. Committing myself to a challenge that was guided by others, *who had been there*, enlightened me to the fact that I could do anything. We joked that weekend about how happy a bear might have been if he had stumbled onto a group of handicapped campers. "Hmmm, let's see, I'll eat this one first...then that one over there…then that one transferring away…not much meat on this one."

Along with A.D.A.P.T. champions Bob and Stephanie Kakfa, we had established a camp for physically challenged kids called EZJ Ranch, which was located on private property near Nacogdoches, Texas. The owner had poured concrete sidewalks throughout the property, which allowed the kids access to the facilities. The three-acre lake was the highlight as we fished, kayaked and sailed each day.

One day Shorty and I checked the "trot line" and became aware of something large, further down the line. As we inched our way along, we discovered a huge turtle hooked through the mouth that had drowned. We removed it, placed it onto the bottom of the boat and headed back to the dock.

I had transferred out of the canoe and was encouraging the kids to head up for supper when Shorty informed us that he thought he saw one of the turtle's eyes flitter. As we turned around, Shorty picked up the turtle and placed its head into his mouth and blew. Surprisingly, the turtle's neck swelled up so Shorty blew again. After four or five blows, one of the arms of the turtle twitched, then another, then the back legs began to move. Happily resuscitated and wondering what had happened between eating a small fish and being kissed by a paraplegic in a canoe, the turtle freely wiggled all of its limbs. Shorty then placed him back in the water and off he went.

If I had not personally seen this, I would not have believed it, but I swear to you, it happened. To pre-approve this for publication, I called Shorty and read him the story. After asking him if my recount was correct, he replied, "What are you talking about, what box?" The point here isn't the type of "roll modeling," but the example of outside the box thinking. It is our shared responsibility to look at the world with every possibility of contributing, of figuring out a way to improve things, even if it means…well, I'll leave the type of contribution up to you.

> With all of our running and all of our cunning,
> if we couldn't laugh, we'd all go insane.
> ❋ Jimmy Buffett

Chapter Seventeen

Tennis Lessons

*Nothing can bring you peace but the
triumph of principles.*
✹ *Ralph Waldo Emerson*

Rehearsed Success

Whether it's Andre Agassi, Bill Clinton or Julia Roberts, an expert handles himself with a comfort level that is misleading. To the pedestrian, it seems he performs without effort. But the performer knows he has spent most of his life rehearsing for that exact point in time.

Take Pete Sampras for example. As he is about to hit a forehand volley, at the last minute, he pulls his racket back and lets the ball go by, which lands an inch beyond the baseline. How does he know it's going out? It's easy. He has seen five hundred million balls travel along that exact same path. He *knows* where the ball will land before it's half way there. Whether muscle or mental memory, establishing a *familiar track* is principle for performance.

With dominating authority, Kai Shraymeyer, the great German wheelchair player, had won six tournaments in a row. Taking the French, Belgian, Dutch, British, Swiss and Israeli Open, he would be named the ITF World Champion in 1993. Kai has a large frame at 6'3", is an amputee due to the removal of his right leg because of a malignant tumor. He plays pressure tennis with his serve and forehand setting the tone for his *rally absent* strategy.

Ranked #1 in the world, he arrived at the U.S. Open in 1993 with one goal in mind, to win the tournament. At the time, I was fourth and drew "Monster Kai" in the semi-finals. This tournament was important to me because if I won, it would be my tenth U.S. Open singles title. In addition, my dad was at the Open for the first time.

Squeaking out a 6–4 third set win, my quarterfinal match against crafty Michael Foulks exposed a deficiency in my forehand. Discussing my dilemma with my coach Dr. Bal Moore, I was asked, "Do you really want to win this championship?" I said, "Sure coach, come on, what do you think?" He said, "The banquet is out, you're back on the court…meet me at 6." We had already been training two hours each morning on top of a singles and a double match, but was I going to question him? Funny thing about training courts at the U.S. Open, during the first few days you can't even get one, but on Friday night, the night of the banquet, trust me, they are all available.

Arriving at the courts, Bal said, "Let's go, it's 2,000 forehands." While all the other players were wining, dining and lying to each other about next year, we hit tennis balls for three hours, one hundred shots at a time. He would say, "Down the line, now cross court, now to the middle, now short." I was sick of them.

The Snow/Schrameyer match was a much-anticipated battle but on that day, we had an additional opponent. Southern California is known for sunny days and rainless Octobers, and in the thirteen-year history of the US Open, it had never rained. But that morning, it was raining. I remember sitting in the lobby of the Hyatt, contemplating the dilemma. We called every tennis facility in Orange County but there were no indoor courts.

As we sipped coffee and stared out across the wet street at the parking garage, *which happened to be the size of an indoor court*, Bal and I simultaneously grabbed our rackets and *pushed forward*. Once inside we located a large space and began hitting "groundies" using a speed bump as a visual for the net. When a security guard approached and said, "You can't hit balls in here," we left and found another parking garage and hit some more. We had prided ourselves in spontaneous innovations over the years, but this set a new mark.

Kai didn't get to "visit" the sport that morning and Bal and I won the semi-finals over the German in an upset 6–4, 6–3 victory. We went on to defeat "boy wonder" Steve Welch in the most lopsided final in the history of the Irvine tournament.

If we want to do it well, whatever it is, nothing replaces mass recitation of the task. At the Paralympics in Atlanta, we exhausted tapes of our opponents and developed a specific game plan for each team. We spent every night in the lobby of our dorm reviewing video, dissecting the strengths and weaknesses of each player and every game situation imaginable. With the meticulousness of a defense attorney going over every possible question, our practices were designed around preparation. I remember once, an interview with Joe Montana about "the catch" made by Dwight Clark and how Bill Walsh had made them do that exact play several times that morning…just in case.

> *Repetition is rehearsed success, and although monotonous, breeds familiarity and confidence.*
> ✳ *Dr. Ballard Moore*

False Pride

Stories have mesmerizing power. From an early age they grab our attention. Like a page in a coloring book, a story presents an outline, leaving the personification up to us. A well-told story can influence us like nothing else. Mine are based around sports, travel and the "beauty within adversity" and this one does not stray. While competing in Roermond, Holland, I came across a Polish man who *storied* the true meaning of pride.

Participating on the U.S. wheelchair tennis team, we were seeded #1 at the 1995 World Team Cup and Coach Bal Moore, Brad Parks, Steve Welch and I were not going to lose, even though the French were champions the previous year. Our first match pitted us against Poland, a rookie country, whose athletes at that time had inferior skill and antiquated equipment. Like the tyrannosaurus rex being teased by the little white goat in the movie *Jurassic Park*, the Polish would only activate our appetite. I drew a guy named Peitor and easily won the first set 6–0. I remember my feelings about my match and the *portrayed* aplomb of the #2 player in the world. Being "surrounded by me," I had employed the psychological countenance needed to overwhelm an opponent.

Ahead 5–0 in the second, I began to empathize with the enemy, so I intentionally double faulted the last two points, making the score 5–1. I had a student ask why tennis players do this and I recalled what Vietnam veteran Joe Moss once told me. He said, "It's the same reason soldiers pick up every casualty of war, no matter what the risk; one day your butt may be in the same situation."

This time though, it backfired. Pietor may not have been ready for a world championship but he knew about pride. It didn't dawn on me as he double faulted the first time, and I still hadn't a clue when he hit the next ball out by several feet. But when he double faulted the next two points and gave me the game and the match, it was clear. At first I wondered, "What's he doing, why would he deny my gift?" But as I approached the net to shake his hand, I noticed no smiles of respect, there were no congratulations on his face. He held my hand for a long moment.

He didn't speak any English and I don't speak a word of Polish, but with his eyes he firmly said, "I know who you are, Mr. Randy Snow, world champion from the great country of America, and I respect your skill and what you have done for our sport. But there is no honor in anything free. Show me the respect I deserve by beating me with everything you have. Even if I lose, this effort is worth more to me than your charity."

> *True pride is an essential ingredient in being a balanced and complete person.*
> ✳ *John Kniffen*

Sacrifice

With history that is beyond belief, Israel is an uncommon country. Not unlike other Middle Eastern regions, it is hot, fast-paced, "type A," passionate and alive. The Wailing Wall and the mosques are icons of two of the oldest religions in the world, which are located not more than 500 meters from each other. Surrounded by people who want their land, the Jews live each day in earnest, accepting the fact that at any moment their businesses, families and plans could take a different path.

As I write, they are again in conflict with the Palestinians, which if a solution did exist, it certainly would have been in place by now. I guess there is always hope. While driving between modern Tel Aviv and the ancient holy city of Jerusalem, one can witness scud missile crash sites and remnants of the Yom Kippur War. Regardless of sport, discipline or disability, as a result of the 1972 Munich tragedy, Jewish sports teams have armed guards that accompany them wherever they go. I rode with their basketball team during a competition in Holland once and we took a different way to the gym every day. Their struggle extends further back in time than most of us realize.

Conversing with my friend, Israeli team physician Dr. Rueven Heller at the Paralympics in Sydney, I said, "The security here is tight, isn't it?" Perturbed, he looked at me and said, "Obviously Randy, you have never lived in conflict." He informed me that he carried two telephones at his side. The one on his left was for the Israeli team and the one on his right was from home. While watching CNN that morning, he witnessed three Jewish reserve soldiers being tossed from a second story window of a police station in Jerico and beaten to death by an unruly mob. With the knowledge that his son was in the army reserve, the phone on his right side rang. He said, "Imagine my prayers before I answered the phone."

When he heard the voice on the other end, he was relieved to find out that is was his son's. From the haven of Amsterdam, his son had left Israel and was calling to say he was OK, but asked if his dad would call "Momma" and let her know. Reuven immediately called his wife and found her sobbing on the other end. She said, "Reuven, have you seen the television?" He informed her of their son's phone call. I was told this one hour after it happened.

The first time I arrived in Israel, I was very excited. Their patriotism was immediately clear as, the moment our wheels touched down at Ben Gurion Airport in Tel Aviv, the entire plane gave an ovation. Having never experienced this before I was so energized, I decided to take in this land and push between the airport and my hotel in Ramat-Gan. From the window of the El Al 757 it only appeared to be a few miles, but many people at the airport said, "It's very far, are you sure you want to do this?" I just thought they were being over-protective, so I insisted and headed out.

As I was pushing along the main road, a man pulled along side of me in an old French car and offered me a ride. He didn't speak much English but informed me that the hotel I was attempting to get to was much further than I thought. Having already pushed three miles, I gave in and trustingly transferred into his vehicle. We surprisingly drove another 12 miles. We finally pulled right up to a large group of people at an outdoor reception honoring sponsors of the tournament. As I was transferring out of this kind gentleman's vehicle, it was obvious there was a problem. The problem wasn't that I had concerned several people at the airport by turning down my ride or that I had almost stranded myself on a freeway in the middle of Israel. The real problem was *my driver was Lebanese*. I have nothing against Arabs but it isn't a good idea to arrive as the guest of honor at a Jewish party with an Arab escort.

While attending the Israel Open Wheelchair Tennis Championships, I was exposed to the *definition of sacrifice*. The first morning of the tournament, we gathered at the rendezvous area at the Hyatt in Jerusalem to board the transportation van to the Israeli Tennis Center in Ramat-Sharon. As this dented and dusty old Volkswagen bus pulled up, a man with polio limped out and in broken English with a Hebrew accent said, "Me Avi, transportation coordinator, I take you tennis center." Avi worked full time as the Transportation Coordinator for the Israel Sports Center. He would transport patients during the week, then take time with his wife and 7 children on the weekends.

Throughout the week, players from all over the world would transfer into his bus and leave their chairs outside. Avi would then lift each one, strap it to the luggage rack on top and away we would go. Upon arrival, he would limp out of the bus, untie and unpack the chairs, then load up another group and depart. Tournaments run four to five days and Avi carried out this responsibility several times each day…gimps in…chairs up…chairs down…gimps out.

On the way to the courts on Super Saturday (Super because it's the day of the men's semi finals and the women's final matches) I said to Avi, "I bet you're going to take a long vacation after this." He said, "No vacation, this is holiday." Bewildered, I asked him why he was using his vacation time to truck a bunch of self-centered athletes and their equipment all around Jerusalem. He said, "You must enjoy, be proud of Israel." He conveyed that it was very important for their guests to know that Israel was a good place, and that if it took using his vacation time to get this message across, his family would understand. I was moved by his patriotic sacrifice. For the rest of the tournament, I referred to him as "Melech (King) Avi."

Integrity

> *Doing the right thing is easy, knowing what the right thing is, is the hard part.*
> ✳ *John F. Kennedy*

Drawing parallels to the real world, outings for people who have experienced accidents offer supervised "practice situations" for them to begin the transition back into life. Random curbs, ramps, slopes, tables, car transfers, bathrooms, and an oblivious society are dealt with in a mentored environment.

One of the most difficult things I remember while at Craig Hospital was the blatant curiosity of the able-bodied population, staring as if we weren't there. My first outing probably should have been a quiet place, void of masses of people but my therapists always *pushed forward*. My first outing wasn't a garden or a restaurant or a visit home. My first outing was Monday Night Football. The TR department took us to Mile High Stadium to watch the Denver Broncos. Concerning people staring, recreational therapist Joe Gomez said, "If you don't look at them, you won't see them looking at you." Sounds trite but I still use it today.

I recall hearing a past patient who "rehabed" at Sharp Rehabilitation Center tell the story of being on a similar outing at the Holiday Bowl football game in San Diego. To start the game, several parachutists fell from the sky as entertainment for the fans. With any high risk sport there is always an accompanying chance of injury. Unsuccessfully partnering gravity, one of the jumpers came in too hard and crashed onto the field. The impact broke his back and traumatically damaged his spinal cord, which was witnessed by 60,000 people. Jokingly one of the spinal cord injuries on the outing said, "That guy is probably going to be my roommate." After stabilization of the injury, ironically, three weeks later, the parachutist was transferred to his room.

Over 300 athletes from around the world attend the U.S. Open each year. To win a title is an ultimate accomplishment. For an ephemeral moment you are the best in the world. But the next day, the win was yesterday. I won the Men's U.S. Open Championship in 1990 defeating Laurent Giamartini from France in a tiebreaker in the third set. I received a small check and a big Rolex. Working at Lakeshore Hospital, I was scheduled to be in the following morning so I booked a red-eye flight back to Birmingham. As I flew, I regretfully remembered I had a tennis lesson scheduled about an hour after I was to land with a twenty-seven year old stroke victim named Margie.

With my tennis bags on top of my chair, I pushed through the parking garage, thinking I really didn't want to teach that lesson. I was exhausted and had planned on going to the office to carry out a few tasks, then head home to enjoy the congratulatory calls and interviews that would be taking place throughout the day.

As I was about to cancel the lesson, *integrity* happened. I was the best tennis player in the world the day before and I felt I deserved that day off, but Margie needed me more than I needed a day off. In reality she didn't need me. She needed to show up and face her own *final*. I was only the tournament director.

As with any of us in a leadership moment, we must know what must be done, make the effort and *play our championships*. In a rare unselfish moment, I set my ego aside and taught the lesson, never telling her about my win. What was significant to me didn't fit into the challenges she faced that morning.

> *Wisdom knows what path to take, integrity takes it.*
> ✳ *Paralympic champion Nancy Olson*

Don't Just Do Something, Sit There

> *They didn't love me because I killed quickly,*
> *they loved me because I won the crowd.*
> ✳ *Proximo*, The Gladiator

Too many tournaments had placed me into mental overcast. I had let all those years cloud life's real substance, masking the reason performers perform. So I was missing the environment that was typically Dutch, as Holland performed all around me with its canals, wind mills, bicycles, stroopwaffel, Van Goghs, and the cheeriest people ever.

Since we had won our two singles matches, we were guaranteed gold in the 1995 World Team Cup, defeating our usual adversary France. We had almost achieved our goal of dominating the competition by not losing a set. Only the insignificant doubles remained, which we played simply for the crowd. Steve Welch and I were matched against Laurent Giamartini and Abde Naili on center court in front of 3,000+ fans. We always liked beating the French because...is there a better reason?

I remember in 1971 going back to the car with my dad after the Texas Longhorns lost to rival Texas A&M. The Aggie fans were teasing us abusively. Especially as a ten-year old, the ribbing struck a direct path to my heart which "burned uncomfortable." I remember my father telling me the teasing was really a compliment, that they were enjoying the win because our football team was good. For someone who bleeds burnt orange, those were soothing words. With the French, it was the same. There was always much satisfaction in defeating Laurent because he was the consummate wheelchair tennis professional.

We had won the first set of the match 6–3, but were down 3–4 in the second. Coach Moore was lecturing us during the changeover but our error management was absent. Wheeling back on the court, I said to Steve, "Come on now, let's win this thing in two and get out of here." Steve pondered my advice, then after the next point said, "I don't know, look around, there are 3,000 people watching us and this doesn't even count. I'd rather be here than anywhere." He wanted to lose the set intentionally so we could play a third and "stay on stage."

I recall another time when during the changeover, I was secretly asked by the director of the Israel Open to slow my winning pace because the Mayor of Jerusalem had not yet arrived for the awards ceremony. Giving in to his request I "hit a slump," then, in a tiebreaker in the second, was informed he had arrived where I went on to "play well" and won. In Holland though, I was the veteran and was supposed to have the wisdom to put matches like this in perspective, so *youth* like Welch could learn. As I replayed his comment and scanned those faces, I knew he knew. The mosaic of a crowd looking right at you is sexual. I said, "OK, I'm on board. I won't miss any shots but I'll stop hitting winners." Coach Moore immediately knew that we were throwing the second set. Metaphysically, he embraced Steve's philosophy and with a level of enjoyment sat back to watch the third. We *lost* the second 6–4, then won the third set 6–2.

Whether living pretty or living brave, there is nothing more important than enjoying the moment.

Make a Stand

I had won several U.S. Open titles on my own but felt in order to improve my game I would have to do something extra. I have said before, it isn't the work that makes someone great, it's the extra work. Ben Hogan said, "You have to train till your hands bleed." Schrameyer, Giamartini, Parks and Connell were closing in and I wanted to stay on top. After meeting Dr. Bal Moore in Birmingham in 1989, we decided we would form a partnership and work together. With the goal of making me better and growing our sport, I would help him with the minutiae of wheelchair tennis and he would bring to me his vast tennis knowledge, refine my game and make me a teacher. We have been together ever since.

In 1991 I was awarded the first ITF World Champion award of wheelchair tennis. Concurrently, Bal was selected as the men's wheelchair tennis coach for the Paralympics that would travel to Barcelona, Spain. We were the premier combination, #1 player in the world and U.S.A. men's tennis coach. We were the team to beat and everybody knew it.

We had arrived at Val Debron Tennis Center where Marc Rosset of Switzerland and Jennifer Capriati of the United States had won their gold medals just two weeks prior. Noticing ball kids exiting the pro shop, we checked in to pick up our meal tickets. Spying an attractive article of clothing on one of the volunteer ball kids, I attempted to avoid the late trade rush by prematurely exchanging one of my spare USA jackets. The ball boy agreed yet regretted the decision throughout the competition and unsuccessfully tried to invert the deal.

As we entered the pro shop and approached the registration desk, I said, "I am Randy Snow and would like to pick up my meal tickets." Bal said, " I would like to get my coach's tickets as well." Jaime Carlos, the director of tennis for the Paralympics, who also served as the director for the Olympics said, "Mr. Snow, your tickets are here, but I'm sorry, there are no tickets for the coach." I thought for a moment, allowing myself to immerse in my status as world #1, then tossed my tickets up on the desk and said, "If the coach doesn't eat, I don't eat." This was a bit risky since a good relationship with event staff is key. Survival favors like additional laundry service, expedited racket stringing or extra practice time can definitely help a campaign. It doesn't behoove one to start out on the wrong foot.

But I felt a stand was necessary. It wasn't that we would be without food because the cafeteria at the village was open 24/7, but due to the layout of the venues, the one-hour bus ride would be very inconvenient. Agitated, we left the building. Since there is no coaching in the Paralympics, we were going over the signals we might use during the tournament when on our way to the bus stop, we heard someone running. As we turned, we saw Mr. Carlos coming behind us and as he arrived he said, "Big mistake, big mistake, we found coach's tickets."

To this day we are the only men's team to have won the gold medal in singles and doubles in Paralympic tennis. Adding to the lore, I'll ask Pierre Fusade, did we use our signals? Incidentally the ball boy became an instant hero.

It is human nature to take our friends for granted, but we must be reminded to make a stand and defend the people who support us. In siding with her little brother in a spat with a neighborhood girlfriend, my six-year old Godchild, Hali, said, "I'm getting more than I'm giving."

HTL

If winning doesn't matter, then why is there a scoreboard in every gym in America?
✳ *Legendary Kentucky basketball coach Adolph Rupp*

My speeches are about being an "effort-based" competitor, avoiding regrets and doing the best job possible, but in me there exists an internal drive that is determined to avoid second place at all costs. Jim Moortgat, tennis coach at NCAA Division I Boise State, often used the acronym HTL, which represents a champion's bottom line. He used to say, "Somewhere, someone is working harder than you. In order to win you have to Hate To Lose." Whether psychologically or physiologically, for me the pain of losing doesn't last as long as it used to. It wasn't the only thing I sought during my career, but winning was a major part. Watching my opponent receive a trophy, a check and make an acceptance speech, *microwaved* my blood.

Bal's tennis team had just lost the Alabama Junior College Championships. As the bus crossed the Talapoosa River on the way home, he made the driver stop and demanded that everyone get off and Coach Moore said, "Bring that trophy with you." At the edge

192

of the bridge he obliged each team member to place a hand on the trophy and on "three," they hurled the second place trophy over the side. Initially the team was in shock, but as the trophy sank to the bottom of the river, the tennis team learned that second place trophies were not acceptable.

After hearing several rumors of the incident, the Athletic Director at Jefferson State called Coach Moore into his office and inquired as to the whereabouts of the trophy. Bal explained what had happened and after fielding a token reprimand, was instructed to buy a brand new trophy and place in the trophy case. There it sat, virtually unnoticed, and after eight years, the Athletic Director finally transferred to a different school. With the memory of an elephant, Bal obtained the key, took out the trophy and tested the waters by hiding it in a closet for six months. Unnoticed, Coach Moore then took the trophy by himself back to the Talapoosa River, stopped at the same place on the bridge and threw it in. There are two second place trophies in the Talapoosa River.

In another story, we were devastated after losing the World Team Cup in Austria. Winning the first 10 years of its existence, the United States had dominated the competition. Some say there was a great rivalry between us and the French but I ask you, is there a rivalry between a hammer and a nail? We knew 1994 would be a "transition year" with me playing a #2 role, Welch as the new #1 and Brad Parks in doubles, but we never thought we would lose.

After promising Coach Moore for two days that the finals would be played inside, the crafty French captain and coach Pierre Fusade convinced the director to switch the matches from the faster indoor courts, to the slower outside battery that benefited the frogs. Steve lost the #1 singles to Giamartini, I won my singles over Naili, but as the '92 Paralympic gold medal team, Brad and I lost the doubles.

Unfortunately for the trophy case at the USTA office, Coach Moore was responsible for delivering the award. The second place trophy, awarded to the United States for the 1994 World Team Cup, is probably still on that piano in the lobby of the Hotel Tirol in Innsbruck being admired by passing hotel guests as an en vogue decorative piece. HTL. Period.

SECTION THREE

FROM MY CHAIR

Chapter
Eighteen

Opening

They had been warned to locate the wheelchair users on the first floor, *just in case of an emergency*, but what were the odds? A fire, no way, it won't happen…and if it does, with all the employees…there will be plenty of help.

So when the fire alarm went off at 5:15 a.m. at the Omni Hotel in Dallas, we hoped the voice coming over the loud speaker would relieve us and say, "Sorry folks, someone inadvertently pulled a lever, it's a false alarm." After all there were 150 wheelchair tennis players from around the world staying on varying levels of this high-rise hotel.

"Ladies and Gentlemen, this is not a test, we have a fire, please evacuate your room to the nearest stairwell and exit to the ground floor. Do not use the elevators." For the next few hours we grabbed whomever we could to help us, and for the players from the upper floors, it was quite a ride. Can you imagine what the fire department thought as they pulled up? People in wheelchairs all over the place and most of us with just a towel in our lap. "Are all of you handicapped?" "No sir, this is a huge sensitivity awareness exercise in how hotel employees interact with naked disabled consumers. We're just temps. Of course we are all…handicapped?"

"Wait a minute, to tell you the truth sir, we're not sure if we are handicapped, invalid, abnormal, disabled, deformed, diseased, spastic, activities limited, physically challenged, crippled, mobility impaired, gimpy, shriveled, crooked, or Special Olympians, but whatever you want to call us, sir, we can't walk and definitely don't like steps."

How do I write this? How can I put it into words? What can I tell you about being in a wheelchair? Unless you have been in one, trust me, whatever you think is incorrect. I know; you have a friend in one or your sister or your dad or your brother-in-law is in one…or you were in one…for two weeks. It won't suffice, you don't know. It is *paradoxically* demeaning and enlightening, all *rolled* into one. The "academic metaphor" provides us a Bachelors degree in acceptance, a Masters in adapting and a Ph.D. in dealing with ignorance.

Spending 30 minutes in a chair in a mall or at an airport is recommended, and to a degree, will certainly help you understand. But to truly know is difficult to explain without living in our seats. I'm sure it's similar to being pregnant or a college-educated Hispanic and constantly mistaken as manual labor being or being a cancer survivor. No one really knows unless he has spent time in that particular situation.

Make note that in no way am I intending to speak for others. Even though I have interacted with many, I do not pretend to know anything about other *characteristics*, visible or not. I have never had an attendant help me with a bowel program, used the audio sensor in an elevator to determine which floor I'm on, or had a son pass away to Duchenne's muscular dystrophy. I am a paraplegic who had an accident at a young age, lived most of my life as a wheelchair athlete and am very lucky to be independent in daily living skills. *My perspective is only mine.*

You will read of many different feelings. Certainly in my life there would have been these emotions. But the quality, severity and intensity to which they exist, and their *concentration of discovery*, has given them magnified impact. I wouldn't have had the same levels of anger, laughter or enlightenment if I had lived my life with the use of my legs. I believe this is a good thing.

Finally, my feelings and perspectives have existed at one time or another and are not *definitive of how I feel or who I am*. Today I attain onward levels of perspective. Sometimes I do exactly what I ask people not to do and other times, I display patience that comes from where, I don't know about. A book's perspective is frozen in time.

After winning my tenth U.S. Open Tennis Championship, I was being interviewed over the phone in my hotel room by a sports writer from the *LA Times*. In commenting on how life had changed for the disabled, I said, "It's like the evolution of a language, it takes generations for us to truly witness the change, but it's moving." As I talked about how far we had come and how wonderful it was to win the U.S. Open, a spasm kicked off my bladder causing me to pee all over myself. I was the best tennis player in the world and peeing on myself at the same time. By the way, in inverse irony, to reduce the chance of urinary tract infections, people with spinal cord injuries are the only beings that wash their hands *before* they pee. Who wouldn't want to miss an impromptu bladder spasm, yet I wouldn't want to trade participating in the opening ceremonies of the Paralympics in Sydney in front of 100,000 light-flickering fans, either? What a *paradox*!

All people in wheelchairs, or in life for that matter are not the same. There are angry gimps and door mat gimps and denial gimps and actualized gimps. I even had a wheelchair tennis student who was a "psychosomatic gimp", who just woke up paralyzed one day, because life was too competitive. There are lots of gimps with many perspectives. From many of the windows of society, living with a disability seems to be a negative experience. There is a great deal of negativity. Conversely though, the lessons, the fight and the experiences are coveted. Most of the disabled people I know agree they would want the same life they have now, only with their legs. This definitely lends testimony to the quality of life we have created.

No, I wouldn't trade my life for the use of my legs for anything in the world...well, I might trade for a few years of my life...OK, I would trade...for...just about anything. Paul, who was injured in a parachuting accident and I, came up with a deal for God. We agreed not to ask for the "whole ball of wax," we wouldn't ask for miracles. But if we had just one favor, we thought we would ask for our legs for one day a month...just twenty-four hours. *Piss on the fire and call the dogs* because that conversation invited some interesting discussion. We listed a plethora of things we would love to do and of course sex was unanimously first.

Several hundred *second choices* were discussed which included walking through the woods, fly fishing in a foot of water in a river, tossing our kids high into the air and catching them and running on the beach. We missed stopping at a store and running in for *anything*, stubbing our toe, walking to the top of a hill, slow dancing with a woman, standing to pee, feeling blue jeans, washing the top of our car and many more. But our real concern wasn't what we would do. Our worry was that it might create a negative reminder of what it was like and eliminate the adjustment we had made, making the other twenty-nine days absolutely miserable. We quickly got over that worry though and agreed to welcome the deal if it were ever offered.

Certainly changing light bulbs, getting lint out of the dryer, reaching for something, turning off the low battery indicator in a smoke detector at 4 a.m., straightening crooked paintings and dealing with throw rugs, extension cords and a shower head that has been redirected by a guest who stayed in your house, definitely take on a new meaning.

A physical disability will expose who the person really is. If they had issues like addictive behaviors, they may worsen before

they get better. Some become very angry or withdraw. Others realize the *break* (again, pun intended), accept and immediately inte-
grate. Through a great deal of work, marriages can be better than
before. More times than not, they end in difference with able-
bodied person saying, "This isn't who I married." Sex will be different. Sex will definitely be different. And just like everybody else
in life, each gimp will want a little more. The vent-dependent quad
will aspire to breathe on his own, the breathing quad wishes he had
hands, the para wishes he could control his bladder and the conti-
nent double amputee wishes he had a knee.

Having a disability reduces the sympathy level for other discriminations. An able-bodied person observes an accident and says
"Oh my." We witness the same accident and say "Oh." Bruce
Horsnby said it best with the title of his song "That's Just The Way
It Is." Sarah, who is able-bodied, worked for a wheelchair manufacturing company for many years. She had been around long
enough to know the "hidden treasures" of living a life with a physical disability. When her daughter was born without an arm (which
is a minor limitation), most of her friends were very distressed,
and some even said, "We will pray for her." Sarah was disgusted.
People who pray for a person without an arm should be prayed
for.

Sympathy shouldn't be misconstrued with empathy. It isn't
that we aren't sympathetic, but from our experiences, we have an
understanding in *real terms* that life is life and will be dealt with one
way or another. Hidden disabilities like sarcasm or anger or low
self-esteem are more difficult because people can continue to live
incognito; they aren't forced to do anything about them. This allows them to painfully function without growing.

> *I love mankind; it's people I can't stand.*
> ✳ *Charles Shultz*

The worst part about being in a chair has nothing to do with
the chair but with *some* of the people around the chair. Frequently,
there seems to be this obligation to mollify our situation. We don't
mind the compassion or help but only if we need it, not because we
are in wheelchairs. Some say, "You should be more grateful, we are
only trying to help." Can you imagine going up to someone who is

bald and publicly offering education on hair transplants? Or how about encountering someone obese who is waiting for a plane and anonymously offering to help council them about their weight? And what if you had to endure eight people a day offering diet advice. "Sorry ma'am, I was just trying to help. Boy is she angry about her weight problem." Do you see? What makes the "do gooder" think they are the only one offering? For the wheelchair bound it is ubiquitous. It isn't the help we mind; *it's the frequency that it happens*. I know it's my social responsibility to display patience and tolerance, but doesn't the correlative faction have some reciprocation, some educational responsibility as well.

Coming towards me out of a Borders Bookstore, I saw a little girl and her grandmother, so I moved aside to let them pass and held the door for them. The little girl said "Thank you," followed by the grandmother who said "Oh, I'm sorry." This incident represents the spectrum of attitudes of the able-bodied population. Why did the grandmother say that? What is she sorry for, not opening the door for me, not opening the door for her granddaughter, putting me in the difficult situation of having to open the door for them? I am very confused by this. Every time an adult says to a child, "Don't stare" or "Watch out," that child will wonder for the rest of its life what is wrong with that person. I know. Let it go, what's the big deal, mountain out of a molehill, but it's easy to say when it only happens to you once or a hundred times. Try it times a million.

> *We are either be lavishly pitied or lavishly admired,*
> *yet we want neither, we just want to be.*
> ✳ *Barry Corbit*

I don't want to peddle the musings of an "angry cripple," because for the most part, people are supportive and compassionate in their dealings. But the *chore* of changing existing paradigms seems analogous to a salmon swimming against a swiftly flowing stream. At some point the salmon must think, "Where is all of this coming from…does it ever end?" Having vented here, I must confess, today I saw an exhausted Hispanic woman in her dirty work clothes, waiting at the bus station with her long sleeve shirt buttoned to the collar in 98-degree weather. I paused and stared, and when she looked at me, I looked away for a moment, then visually returned, pitying her...for what reason...why?

> *...and I wept to see him suffer, although I didn't know him well...*
> ✳ *Carol King, Tapestry*

If we could hold a seminar for all the children of the world and educate them to the fact that a disability is just another human characteristic, like moles, red hair or sarcasm, there would be no more "stream to swim against." The awareness would perpetuate, being passed down from generation to generation. I believe we must continue to educate the able-bodied population and pave the way for those who follow. The solution does not lie in a passive or aggressive approach, but in *an assertive one.*

Every Life Is a Story

I was doing a motivational speech at a rehab center in California and met a newly injured woman who was pregnant. It was obvious her accident happened after her pregnancy and I couldn't help but ask her about her path to this place.

She said she had gotten out of her car carrying groceries in a nefarious neighborhood and all of a sudden a car drove by with several boys inside. As the car approached, the gunshots began to ring out and one struck her in the back, dropping her to the hot concrete, groceries spilling out everywhere. Falling into shock she said she remembered being very disappointed about the broken eggs, trying to "gather them up" on the hot sidewalk in blood, attempting to avoid injuring her unborn child.

She was transferred to rehab and began the long journey of starting over, of crawling again just as her unborn child would soon be doing. After a few months she felt she just couldn't go on, worrying about the baby, her other two children and about her husband who had recently abandoned her. He told her he just couldn't deal with the wheelchair.

One evening she took the elevator to the fifth floor of the center to transfer out the window to their death, but she wasn't strong enough to make it up onto the windowsill. For the next month her secret motivation was to complete her therapy and become strong enough to transfer up onto the ledge. During the day-by-day progress, she found value in her life and came to realize that she was going through it for a purpose. She became ready for what God intended for her to do.

In another case I met a man with a spinal cord injury from a motorcycle crash. He had worked for a large computer company for many years and as a gift to himself, bought a large "road cruiser." On the way home, he lost control of the bike, skidded into a fence and broke his neck. The injury was untimely and devastating; however he was left with valuable hand function and triceps, which are golden to a quadriplegic. These are the muscles that not only allow a person to push their wheelchair but also transfer, lift their body, and function independently. But he elected to withdraw from any more risk taking and press his wife to care for him. Even though others with the same disability are raising children, flying airplanes and teaching school, he will not make the attempt. Dealing with a major change is personal. It depends on many factors of past experiences. It's all a choice.

I met a young man in a small town not too long ago whose injury warranted the investigation of negligence. A friend of mine with the exact same accident was awarded a large sum. The family was economically challenged but safely grounded in love and family values. After the attorney had done his research, he drew up a contract, not guaranteeing anything, but enlightened them of the fact that they had a "good suit." I assumed it was a done deal, they would sign the agreement, the firm would move forward and the family would benefit from the forthcoming capital. I was shocked when months later, the attorney called to inform me they never signed the contract. I never spoke to them again but I'm sure the mom felt the money would complicate their lives, threaten her base, and that she might lose their family integrity. To what, she wasn't sure? The one thing she was sure of was, they were OK the way they were.

Often it is the risk-taking, self-destructive, apocalyptic behavior that delivers the person to the chair. Unfortunately upon arrival, nothing was learned, the characteristics of the individual did not change and their lifestyle stayed the same. There is nothing more harmful than plopping a lump sum of money on top of a smoldering ember of emotional unstableness. I have seen it often, people with injuries and settlements, enabled by money to the point of anesthetization and unhealthy paranoid relationships. Sometimes there is an early check-out. But there are many that have taken their financial blessing and invested it, using the money for what it was intended, making their lives more comfortable.

My brother-in-law works for a high-tech microchip company and attended the first day of a five-day seminar. The lecturer, a world-renowned expert in his field, came out onto the stage, began speaking, and with his first few words revealed severe cerebral palsy. My brother-in-law couldn't understand what he was saying. Later that evening during the evening meal he said, "Honey, I don't know what to do, I can't understand a thing this guy is saying. His words are unrecognizable, they're all over the place." My sister said, "You will be able to understand him soon. You will adapt to your disability."

Maybe we are all disabled since we can't live
in peace with each other.
✳ *Gary Karp*

Chapter Nineteen

Excuse Me?

The following are actual statements made to me over the last 25 years. Some are self-explanatory, others I have prompted, but all reveal some deep embedded attitudes. Enjoy and ponder.

"I was in a wheelchair once for two weeks, and I know what you are going through."

"Do you eat special food?"

"Well you don't look handicapped!"

"Do you sleep in your wheelchair?"

"Your life must be horrible. Have you ever thought about suicide?"

"Do you need a ride?" I was in my racing chair in the country doing a twenty-seven mile workout.

"Slow down, you are going to get a speeding ticket."

"Hey Speedy." I am not a car.

"You aren't going to have kids are you? We already have enough cripples in the world."

"Why would you do that to a kid?" This was made during a discussion about being a dad.

"Are your kids in wheelchairs?"

At dinner with any female wheelchair friend "Are you married?" Frequent.

"Beep-beep-beep-beep-beep-beep." A guy made this comment out loud while I was backing between two tables in a restaurant.

"You are just amazing." For no reason, this statement is made frequently.

"Who takes care of you?"

"Is your wife handicapped?"

"Can you go to the bathroom?"

"Do you still have a penis?"

"What will he have to eat?" A waiter asked my friend this question while we were at the table.

"Will this room be OK for him?"

"Are your legs dead?"

"How come your legs are so shriveled?" A child asked me this during a speech.

"Are you guys here for a convention?" In jest, I usually say, "Yes… yes we are, it is a train wreck convention, it was a really bad one and we get together once a year to process the accident."

"Is that a band instrument?" I was pushing my racing chair in a shipping box.

"You sure are nice for a person in a wheelchair."

"That's a neat little trailer." I was pushing my basketball chair through the airport.

"I'm so glad I am not in your situation."

"I wondered what you would do if I hadn't have been here?" A lady waited for me to get out of my car, opened a door for me at a mall and made this statement.

"And you are so handsome."

"Is that a violin?" I was pushing through the lobby of a hotel carrying my tennis racket bag that said Prince on the side.

"Do you compete in the Special Olympics?" No, but I volunteered once. Want a hug?

"You are pretty good, I bet you could beat me." This comment came from an obese lady while we were riding in an elevator. I said, "You think?"

"You should show your disability a little more respect." A man said this to us after we laughed loudly at Felix's Oyster Bar on Bourbon Street in New Orleans.

"May I help you?" "Want some help?" "Need some help?" "Let someone help you?" "You better get someone to help you." These would be acceptable if I had asked.

After stopping to help a lady change a flat tire where I transferred to the ground to do the work, she followed me to my car and said, "Do you need some help?"

"Someone has to go with you." This was said in Hong Kong at the airport when I said I needed to go the bathroom.

"No...I am sorry, wheelchairs can't go there." I wanted to go to a shopping area in the Frankfurt Airport. I looked down at my wheelchair and said, "Wait here, I'll be right back."

"God will take care of you for doing this." A lady said this to a girl I went to dinner with.

"It is nice of you to go out with him." This was said to a different dinner date by a different lady. The first one didn't date me anymore.

"Does he need much help?"

"You will have to take care of him the rest of your life." My fiancée's mother said this to her. We didn't marry.

"This is a disgrace." Under his breath, a banker quietly said this to his attorney partner as another wheelchair player and I were beating them in tennis.

"Why do you go out there?" Said to us just before going onto the court to play tennis.

"If you would just believe in God, he would help you."

"If you would really try you could walk. No, really try."

"You don't want to walk, do you?"

"You've got to be mentally tough."

"If it had happened to me, I would be walking." A husband said this to his newly injured wife.

"Watch out." A lady in a parking lot yelled this at me. That's all she said.

"Watch it, he will run over you." A mom in a store recently told her kid this. He just stared at me in fear.

"If you kids don't settle down, you are going to be just like him." Trying to settle her kids down, a mother pointed at my friend (a paraplegic) and said this.

"But we don't have any wheelchair customers." A postal clerk made this comment when after scooting up the steps, I asked him why the Post Office didn't have a ramp.

"WHEELCHAIR!" Sometimes this is loudly yelled at security stops at airports to let other staff members know a manual pat down is needed. I'm not a wheelchair.

And finally…"I'm sorry." This is the common wheelchair greeting, which frequently takes the place of "Hello."

I'm Not a Wheelchair

In a bar in New York City in 1984, on a whim I bet my crazy friend Pete $100 he wouldn't take his pants off and wheel the entire length of the club in his underwear. Not only did he do it, no one even noticed. True story. The patrons saw a wheelchair and didn't even notice the *naked* person in it. Unfortunately (fortunately *for Pete's sake*) we are too often viewed as "wheelchairs" rather than people using wheelchairs.

The following stories and comments are from a few that remain afraid or only see the negativity associated with the disability, or that just don't think.

After carrying groceries to the counter in one of the small baskets provided by the store, thinking they are making it easier, the clerk will place the groceries into two bags, then ask if I need help carrying them out. When I say no and inform them that I carried the same amount of groceries in one basket, and to please put them into one bag, they say, "Well I was only trying to help." In my opinion, this statement is an attempt to shift the focus from their laziness and lack of observation to my "negative attitude."

Nervous enough in interacting with the disabled person, occasionally when a store clerk hands over the change after a purchase, the possibility now exists of touching them. It just irritates me when they recoil as their hand makes contact, like paraplegia is contagious. If the change is mishandled and dropped onto the floor, an uncomfortable scene is created for everyone. As quickly as possible, I usually attempt to pick up anything dropped to avoid the nightmare of people involved in bumbling sympathy.

Toilet seats in airports are where men retaliate on their families for being pressured to lift them at home. A million times I have gone into the wheelchair accessible restroom in an airport and discovered urine all over the seat. I can just see them, unzipping their pants and vindictively peeing all over the seat, saying, "Ha, Ha, Ha…TAKE THAT."

People in wheelchairs are very aware of the extra room provided in the accessible restrooms. That is why they are *accessible*. Granted, the odds of a disabled person needing to use the restroom while an able-bodied person *"sneaks a pee"* are very low, but they are designed to meet the needs of mobility impaired person *when they need it*.

I have gone in restrooms to find several stalls open and an able-bodied person in the only gimp stall. When exiting, they usually say, "Oh, sorry." I sarcastically offer the statement, "There sure is a lot of room in there, isn't there?" Unaware (or sarcastically aware), they usually say, "There sure is."

Because I frequently travel with my sports chair, when I discover one of these *"pee sneakers,"* if I am having a bad day, I sometimes place my tennis chair right in front of the door. This makes them struggle with the confinement as I might struggle to get into a narrow stall. I eventually move the chair away and say, "Oh, I'm sorry." If I'm having a real bad day, sometimes I'll pull right into the middle of the urinals, insert my catheter in full view and pee freely. It sounds like a zipper wave moving away from me in both directions.

Flight attendants can be a chronic problem. Their business is to go out of their way to make people comfortable, but with the disabled population, some of them exaggerate as if their patronizing attitude will surely make us happy. If we know anything, we know baby talk and to us, it's "scalding."

After putting my backpack on the back of my chair, a flight attendant once said, "Wow, that's amazing." Why this false dialogue pushes my insecurities, I don't know, but it must be located right on my forehead. Lately, before they can get out the statement, "Do you need some help up the jet way?"…I ask them the same question. Caught off guard, they ponder what I said, which definitely eliminates any more frothiness.

We call it "general accounting principle" transfers, how people in wheelchairs are placed on and off airplanes. It's first in, last out.

Flight attendants who accompany us frequently entertain wheel-chair users when, just before the plane lands, they kindly ask us to wait in our seat until everyone else deplanes. Where do they think we are going? Once I had a flight attendant begin to explain the emergency procedures for disabled passengers by asking if I had ever flown before. Offering a sarcastic "No," I said, "But in case of an emergency, you stay seated and as soon as I get everyone else off the plane, I'll come back and get you. If I have to, I will place you on my back and carry you out myself." Acknowledging my satire, she smiled as I continued, "Listen, if we crash, I assure you, unless I am unconscious, I won't be here."

Once a flight attendant made me sit on a blanket before take-off. She said it was for my safety in case I needed help being carried off the plane. I think she was covering the seat because she thought I might pee. This was a clear case of two-way miscommunication, but I was still very angry. Another time, an airline employee said I absolutely couldn't fly unless I had a companion. I went back up the jet way, made an announcement to the waiting passengers that I couldn't fly unless I had a companion, and asked for volunteers. When she asked me what my companion's name was, I said, "I don't know but he's right over there."

Each airplane has an aisle chair on board for transporting non-ambulatory individuals to the restroom. I asked a flight attendant once if she would get it for me. As she explained this to the other flight attendant, as if I couldn't see them, they both rolled their eyes. They better hope as I do, that one of the 10,000 spinal cord injuries that occur each year in the United States doesn't happen to them.

At a nondenominational church in Hawaii, I had a lady get up during the service, walk across the church and bring me a bible. I said, "No thank you," and she huffed. If I take the bible, I publicly give in to the societal belief that we are helpless. Since I didn't take the bible I have a chip on my shoulder. Where am I supposed to be? Am I being a moron? What happened to my right to get my own bible or to ask for my own bible? Why didn't she offer a bible to any-one else in the building? If these stands are made assertively and in an appreciative way, we challenge existing stereotypes.

The "opening the door" scene can be a bottleneck. I still place it into the "we will ask if we need help" category. Most are amazed when we independently execute the task, saying, "Wow," or "Good for you," but sometimes the gesture can get out of hand, with the able-bodied person more "in the way." I really get a kick out of people holding elevator doors or moving their hand in front of the sensors of automatic doors. I've been on an elevator before that has stopped at another floor as someone gets on. Of course, the first thing they say is, "I'm sorry." Then they say "Which floor?" This is a very interesting statement. Do they think I've been riding up and down, waiting for someone to get on and push the button for me? "Thank you ma'am, the lobby please, I've been trying to get there for an hour." Able-bodied people don't do this for each other.

It's the absurd occasions of ignorance and lack of thought that infuriate a person with a disability. I was at South Padre Island with my family and went to the *Blue Marlin* grocery for some provisions. When I asked a man if he would hand me a can of Old Bay seasoning, he obliged, then patted me on the head and said, "I would do anything for a guy in your condition."

One time a group of us went to a restaurant in Japan and sat down at a table. Although obvious eye contact was made, no one would serve us. We inquired about service and were totally ignored. Finally we asked for the owner. He wouldn't come over to the table. He just stood at the cash register and flicked his hand towards the door, indicating that we should leave. This was downtown Tokyo.

Another time, in Paris, we had to get our able-bodied friend to wave down a taxi because every time the drivers saw that we were in wheelchairs, they would speed away. Once I took a taxi from my hotel in Rome to the airport and the driver was so afraid, he drove over 120 miles an hour and yelled the entire time. I started popping him on the back of the head, demanding he slow down, which caused him to drive faster and yell even louder. When we arrived, he leaped out of the car and literally threw my bags and me out of the cab onto the curb and sped away without being paid.

At a little convenience store in Hong Kong, I couldn't get people to stop breaking the line in front of me. I finally got into a big argument with the last person who cut. It was like I wasn't there. At a tennis clinic, after giving a short lecture, I asked the participants, who were able-bodied coaches, to hop into the chairs and begin learning the sport. One gentleman would not get into a wheelchair and said, "Man, that's bad luck."

I suppose it is the misunderstanding of us that is so scary. Maybe we represent vulnerability in life, which no one wants to acknowledge. The other day I was wheeling through the Austin airport coming up behind a father carrying a baby, with another child walking ahead. As I approached, he loudly said, "Watch out" to his son, who froze causing me to have to adjust, and I almost bumped into him. Angering the father, he yelled at me saying all I had to do was say excuse me. I had just returned from Australia competing for the United States and had been on airplanes for twenty hours and I was tired. I said, "No one had to say anything. It would have been fine. You scare your child when you say watch out." He said, "I understand your anger, asshole, but you don't have to take it out on me, and don't tell me how to raise my kids." Of course now I *was* angry and couldn't have healthy dialogue, *even though our conversation continued*!

We are aware of the fear associated with the interaction with someone with a disability. There is grace in the innocent mistakes and appreciation of the attempts of compassion. Overall, humanity has gone out of its way to genuinely help people in need. This is demonstrated continuously, if we look around us. Mike Haynes told me a story that captures what people can do if they think. He had traveled with an entire group of disabled scuba divers that had just landed in Belize to change planes. The plane they were to board was full of passengers waiting right next door. Rather than carry twenty people off that plane, and onto the other one, the gate director asked the entire plane of able-bodied passengers to switch. No one complained. This represents the supportive attitude I have experienced most of the time as well.

As being uncomfortable can be a problem for some, patience and tolerance can be a problem for me. I am aware. It is my life assignment and I work on it frequently. Our ultimate goal, the way we live our lives, existing to the point of stubborn independence or "supercrip" status, is to make the wheelchair as insignificant as possible...not the person.

Chapter Twenty

Two police officers found an inebriated gentleman lying on the floor of a bar. In an attempt to sober him up, they held him up, then let him go and he fell and hit his head. After carrying him out to their car, they attempted to sober him again by standing him up.

This had the same result, as the gentleman fell forward, hitting his head on the bumper. Now feeling guilty, the officers pulled out his wallet, found his address on his license and drove him home.

They carried him to the door and before knocking, one more time let him stand by himself to try to wake him. This time he fell over the porch and broke his leg. As the gentleman's wife answered the doorbell, the police officers said, "Sorry for bringing your husband home in this condition, ma'am, he wouldn't wake up." She said, "Oh, thank you, did you bring his wheelchair?"

Humorous Snapshots—Statements

In the previous statements I revealed absurd comments. To change the mood, the following "slips" reveal a lighter side. Again, enjoy and ponder.

"You guys go ahead and seat yourself, will you?" This was said to four of us all in chairs, waiting in a restaurant.

"Wait a minute, I'll seat you." This was said to the same four in a different restaurant.

"How does it feel?" A statement offered by a nervous shoe salesman to a friend who had just put a shoe on her prosthesis.

"I saw your leg move!" A kid said this to me during a speech.

"Do you want to fly stand-by?" I would love to.

"You need to make a stand."

"Try crawling before you walk."

"You are walking on pins and needles here."

"I feel like I'm playing a pregnant lady." An able-bodied lady said this to me as she and her able-bodied partner were losing to Susan Finklestein and me. She couldn't decide whether to pity me or play all out. We won the match.

"Wouldn't want to walk a mile in his shoes…would you?" Well, maybe a mile.

"I need you to stand by me, OK?" Sorry, I just can't do it.

"You can run but you cannot hide." It's the contrary mate.

"Randy…you walk your mother down the aisle." Said to me before my sister's wedding. I don't think so.

"Stand up and be counted."

"Just walk it off." A referee said this to me after I was hit in the head with a basketball.

"Sir, wheelchairs aren't allowed to use the escalator." I was already half way down.

"Will you walk the dog while I'm gone?" I would love to.

"Come on in and have a seat." May I have a seat first?

"I stand corrected." Not me.

While warming up hitting heavy-paced-cross-court-forehands, Steve Welch and I heard a guy next to us say to the other tennis player, "Hey man, are you seeing this?"

"The first step is the hardest." No kidding.

"I need to tell you something…are you sitting down?" Give me a second.

"Come on, let's go, it's just a hop, skip and a jump from here." I might be awhile.

"Stand by your word." Can't do it.

"Any landing you can walk away from is a good one." After a bumpy landing, a flight attendant said this to me. She never got it.

"Don't stand for it, OK?" OK.

"I can't stand it anymore." Neither can I.

"Yes, we take walk-ins." What about roll-ins?

"Why don't you sit on it for awhile?" No problem.

Struggling to climb into the boat after water-skiing, Red, who is a paraplegic, heard a guy cruising by in another boat say, "Hey stupid, there is a ladder in the back."

And my favorite…"Please remain in your seat until the aircraft comes to a complete stop." Well, since you have asked politely…OK!

Humorous Snapshots—Life

> *I recall an article announcing Mattel's attempt at accessing the huge disabled market with the introduction of "Wheelchair Barbie," but she couldn't get into her "Barbie Doll House" because the doors were too narrow. Accessibility issues are omnipotent.*

I was making a sales call on a client who had inquired about getting her wheelchair maintained. After knocking on her door, a lady about 60 years old answered, then let me in. I found out she had lost her legs to diabetes and since she was without family, had recently downsized her residence from a large home to the apartment in which she currently lived.

After some small talk, I started to shut the door but she asked me to leave it open for her cat. I said, "What's your cat's name?" She said "Whiskey." I said, "Whiskey is a unique name for a cat." She agreed and said there was some question as to her character when, for the first two weeks, she would leave her apartment, which was located on the outside of the complex, wheel around in the courtyard and yell, "Whiskey, Whiskey." In later conversations, some of her neighbors said that before they knew she was a resident, they thought she was a "no-legged" street lady who kept wandering into their apartment complex, yelling out her drink of choice. But none of them had the heart to call the police.

Our wheelchair basketball team had pre-boarded the plane and settled in. Arriving at her row, a lady informed David, who was sitting in the aisle, that her seat was next to the window. Doing the best a paraplegic "paralyzed from the nipples down" could do, he wiggled and wobbled, which really didn't do anything, then said, "Here you go." The lady considered him a jerk and to the best of her ability, squeezed by him to her seat. Just before she sat down, in a snub, she said, "Do you mind placing my coat in the overhead compartment." Offering a sincere, "Sure, no problem," he took her coat, did a little hook shot and successfully landed the fur right into the compartment. She didn't speak to him the rest of the flight. She finally became aware that David was in a wheelchair when she saw him at the baggage area, where she *drooled* apologies.

Gimp virgins are individuals who have never had any real interaction with anyone with a disability. Their *lack of experience* produces a very uncomfortable state, which can be disarmed by a patient and sensitive gimp. This "first time" experience can affect how the able-bodied will think of the disabled for years to come.

I had just received a haircut from a new hair stylist who was a gimp virgin and after she was finished, I was lowered down in the barber's chair so I could transfer into my wheelchair. When I tried to lift my body into my chair, I had difficulty because my feet had fallen under the platform of the barber's seat and were being pressed by the footrest. It was a bit embarrassing when I had to ask her to raise the seat back up, so I could get my feet out from underneath the bar. She turned down my tip.

Human beings are habitual creatures. It's about routines, about making things convenient, and especially for someone just out of rehab. The sooner we groove the process, the quicker we settle into a functional state with the real world. It's in the early risk taking that provides some *exposing* stories.

Julie, who broke her back after falling while performing as a cheerleader at a basketball game, had been home for two months. I know the feeling of wanting to get back to your friends, yet the uncertainty of how you will be received or how you will function physically is unpredictable. The last thing you want to do is to *get caught with your pants down*. This happened to me as I was determined to walk when I got home. Dating myself, I was going up the stairs in my long leg braces at the "foosball hall" and as all my friends came to the door to greet me, I lost my balance and fell in a pile of paralyzed limbs, braces and crutches. I didn't wear my leg braces in public again for a long time.

Julie had a boyfriend before her injury but hadn't gone out with him since she had come home. As soon as she returned home, he made the move to reacquaint and asked her to dinner. Overcoming some early nervousness, everything was going fine until they were about to leave the restaurant. She had excused herself to catheterize and returned through the diner. Arriving back at the table, they headed towards the entrance where the valet had retrieved their vehicle. As she transferred into the passenger seat, she realized that she had been in too much of a hurry in the restroom because when she started to lift her legs into the car, she found her underwear hanging around her ankles.

One time a girl asked me over to her parents' home to enjoy a new hot tub they had just installed. I was a bit nervous since I didn't really know her that well and my nervousness was intensified when she asked her parents to join us. As I sat in the tub across from her father, I noticed he held a very curious and uncomfortable look on his face. I thought it might have been because I was definitely thinking about getting in that hot tub alone with his daughter, but how could he tell? With the sixth paraplegic sense, I employed a "self-check" and began to assess the *paralyzed unknown*. I was shocked when I found my right leg levitating above the bubbles from one of the air sources in the bottom of the tub, which was lightly pushing my foot into the testicles of her father. I wasn't aware of it because I couldn't feel it. Whenever I attempt to explain an embarrassing moment in life, I call it *dancing*. I was doing some *serious dancing*.

In previous stories I have referred to the "self-check." This biological alert reminds a gimp to personally evaluate paralyzed parts of the body. Ask any spinal cord injury, when the "self-check" is neglected, there can be some horrendous consequences, as they had no idea they were in peril.

I went to a company sales meeting for 200 of our employees held in the foothills of the Rocky Mountains in Keystone Colorado. One night we went to a dude ranch, which offered horseback riding, roping, a hayride, campfire singing and a huge meal cooked in "pack-train" style. I attended the roping to witness how "out of character" city folk would look attempting to mimic one of the skills so necessary for that region a hundred years ago.

I had pulled my wheelchair up to the edge of the roping area, and getting very comfortable, I slouched back and tossed my legs out forward with my feet touching the ground. As I watched a friend from Boston embarrass herself, I began to feel a little woozy. Crediting the 10,000-foot altitude of Keystone, I struggled to let the feeling pass. As I waited, it didn't pass. In fact it became worse and I began to feel sick. I couldn't figure out what was happening. Why would I begin to feel sick for no apparent reason?

After paralysis, the remaining communication methods within a body are either through sight, bone reverberation, blood flow, or sensory nerves called "neighborhood sensation." Like delivering a message using the Mississippi River, blood flow communication is definitely the slowest. To ensure that nothing was being done to my body, I began the "self-check," starting with the waist area. I moved down my frame looking for anything glaring. Just below my knees, I was shocked to find about 200 ants, chewing away at my legs. Evidently when I tossed my feet forward, I had placed them right on top of a huge ant bed. I am sure the sensory nerves in my legs were burning up the synapses, yelling "EMERGENCY." Once the last ant was removed, the "venom wave" finally faded. From now on I am more aware of where I place my paralyzed feet.

Another time I was cleaning fish on a cutting board in my bare feet. I was in Southern Louisiana enjoying the marshlands of Danny's Fish Camp on Bayou Lafourche in Golden Meadow. We fish the same water-ways Jean Lafitte actually used to escape after he "privateered" the British and Spanish cutters. Mentally reminiscing how I was going to cook my fish, I was filleting some "specks" and noticed the guts and fish juices dripping through the wooden slats of the cleaning board. Wondering if I was making a mess, I glanced down and saw the tail of a cat. As I looked under the table, I saw this big feline biting on my toes like they were pieces of fish. I quickly shooed the tomcat away and was thankful for my paralysis, because I was pretty certain it hurt.

Speaking at schools is very enjoyable and part of my job responsibility with my company, NoXQS, Inc. I enjoy the honesty of the kids; they are our most important resource. We need to capture them early during their "core belief" years and I attempt to keep their attention the best I can. But the lack of excitement from my audience at Karras Elementary should have been an honest indication that something was wrong. Their gawking stares were out of the ordinary. Continuing on, I just assumed the kids were still settling in.

As I turned to cross the stage, I glanced down at my shin and footrest area and noticed a river of dried blood that started just below my knee and trailed all the way down into my sock. Unknowingly, I had gashed my leg when I closed the door to my vehicle. I have no idea what the kids were thinking but I quickly excused myself, cleaned off the blood, returned and attempted to *dance* my way out of it.

Participating in a camping trip early after my discharge proved hazardous. Intending on warming my hands, when I neared the fire, I wasn't aware that my feet had ended up a lot closer than my hands. After sitting there for an hour or so, I finally withdrew for the evening. In order to keep my feet protected throughout the night, I left my boots on, until the morning. I removed them the following morning and discovered my poor little toes, which looked more like ripe grapes than metatarsals. Aloe Vera leaves were scarce in my house for months after that incident.

Being self-conscious after our injuries is natural. As we re-enter the world, we can't help but notice how we make some people nervous, and out of politeness, attempt to avoid societal infractions. Occasionally I tend to over-do it and sacrifice my personal enjoyment by making sure others around me aren't uncomfortable.

I had been home for about a year and was venturing back into high school and the dating scene. Attempting to make a subtle transfer in public was a big step, yet the opportunity of sitting close to someone of the opposite sex warranted the risk. In the middle of the movie, my focus left my self-conscious mode and steered more towards personal benefit, which was about getting somewhere with my girl. Rather than placing my arm around her shoulders, I opted for her leg. Without making it too obvious, I subtly made the move and placed my hand on her leg. She didn't even respond. With the skill of a sculptor, I delicately moved my hand along her leg, signaling an interest to hold her hand or at least initiate an acknowledgment that my advance met her approval. Still, there was no response. Defeated, I withdrew and violated the "gimp rule of stealth" by looking in the direction of her leg. I was shocked when I discovered that my hand wasn't on her leg; it was on mine.

Town Lake in Austin is one of the more attractive features of the beautiful downtown area. That specific stretch of the Colorado

River is filled with bike paths, landscaping and even a statue of native son, Stevie Ray Vaughan. It is a charming area of the River City. Many locals enjoy kayaking on Town Lake and I am no different. Once I get my kayak into the water, I can independently transfer, leave my chair on shore, and enjoy the same freedom as my able-bodied peers.

Returning after a four-hour trip, I found two police officers and several joggers hanging around my chair. They were looking out into the water. Unsure of their motive, from my kayak, I said, "Can I help you?" One of the police officers said, "Have you seen anyone out there?" I hadn't seen anyone all day so I informed him. He said, "Are you sure?" All of a sudden, it hit me as I realized he was looking for the person that belonged to the wheelchair. Just to be thorough, I said, "Why, what's wrong?" "We are missing someone." I said, "Officer, if you are looking for the person that belongs to that chair, it's mine." The group frustratingly looked at each other then began dispersing. In a relieved voice, he asked, "Next time you go fishing, do you mind leaving a note. We were about to call our divers."

Another time at Town Lake I had taken a date out on my boat for a romantic "hidden cove" picnic. I had left my wheelchair on the dock and wasn't worried because we would be returning in a couple of hours. Anyway, who would steal a wheelchair? Upon our return though, I noticed that my wheelchair was gone. As we scanned the area, I saw it about a hundred yards up on a hill. My friend went up to retrieve it but returned to inform me that it was chained to a post and handed me a note. The note said, "Afraid your wheelchair would be stolen, please call 555-1212 and I will come back and unlock it." I appreciated this person's concern but I still have one question. If I had been by myself, how was I to get that note?

We had been to Corpus to hang out with Julian many times. Credit his settlement, he had the ultimate "para-pad," a gimp bachelor's dream with a pool, weight room, a game room and all accessible. In addition he had a '56 mint condition baby blue Chevy, with some huge motor, a van with a lift and a four-wheeler at our disposal. And he had lots of bucks. These amenities drew the attention of the ladies as well. We loved Corpus. We loved Julian.

Since the van and Chevy were being used, Mark, a paraplegic, and I had *no choice* but to take the four-wheeler to Padre Island, which was located fifteen miles from the house. With a beer or two influencing our decision, foolishly, we were on our way. Without our chairs, it was difficult to convince anyone at the store that we were disabled and needed something from inside. Would you give the time of day to a couple of big guys on the back of a four-wheeler, asking for a favor and stating they couldn't walk?

We finally made it to the beach, where we transferred off our ride and crawled out into the ocean. Either the spirits, or the girth of the borrowed suit, or my paralysis or the swirling surf detached me from my suit, but the next thing I knew, I was naked. In a scuba class once I was totally unaware when my weight belt slipped from around my waist and hung around my feet. Paralysis has no empathy.

Tapping into survival problem solving, which we must develop over the years, Mark found a towel on the beach and we "borrowed it." Attempting to cover as much as possible, I wrapped myself in the towel and we headed for home. After driving most of the distance, we were just about to leave the highway when a Corpus Christi "police cruiser" pulled behind us and turned on his lights. Here were two disabled guys (one wrapped in a towel) without wheelchairs, carrying four beers in a backpack that had just ridden a four-wheeler fifteen miles after swimming at Padre Island. I assume he didn't want to carry us to his police car because after our "lecture," we were released with a promise never to return.

Whether disabled or not, during the initial stages of dating, there is apprehension. Between the interest in the other person and being self-conscious, we can sometimes become distracted from the common routines we ordinarily fulfill.

Although not an athlete, Carol had done more for wheelchair sports in the Dallas area than any other person has. She had absorbed many challenges aside from her birth defect and when she started dating Jay, everyone was excited for the both of them. Since they had attended the same high school, Jay had decided to take Carol to the football playoffs for their first date. Carol said the usual unfamiliarity had been worked through beautifully, with Jay's chivalry clearly impressing her. A couple of times, Jay even helped push Carol. This included a very steep hill where the handicapped seating of the stadium was located.

Continuing with the courtesy after the game, Jay had suggested they wait for the crowd to dissipate before descending down to their car in the parking lot. Carol was absolutely wooed! While they waited and watched the sea of people, Carol's chair began to drift. Thinking her movement was initiated by Jay, Carol kept her hands in her lap as she thought she was being re-positioned by her romantic date. Noticing the slight movement of his date's wheelchair, Jay thought Carol was adjusting for a better view of the exodus of the football fans. By the time they realized that *neither* had control, it was too late, as Carol headed over the side, down the steep embankment to the melange of cars below.

Flying at warp speed, Carol screamed, "JAAAAY!", which prompted Jay to run as fast as he could in an attempt to catch her. With Jay desperately reaching for her chair, Carol crashed into the side of a stopped car, then splattered onto the ground. Imagine the family in the car, looking out of their window at the "human comet" of Jay running after Carol, coming right at them. Fortunately, Carol wasn't hurt, and not only did they go out again, Carol and Jay have been married for 10 years. Incidentally, their second date was at a one-story restaurant.

Humorous Snapshots—Sports

Having dinner the other night, the wife of a friend of mine, who only has one leg, said she finally cured him of the habit of going into the shoe store and asking for 2 boxes of the same shoe. When the clerk wasn't looking, he would switch the right and left shoe in the boxes, creating 2 pair of the same shoe. This left him with 2 remaining challenges; to keep from being discovered while buying the shoes and to make sure he got the right box. This is the same guy who convinced his dry cleaners to give him a discount since they were only cleaning one leg of his pants.

As with the previous stories, the following also invite laughter but with a sports twist.

As wheelchair sports developed in the '80s, as far as sponsorships, we attempted to follow in the footsteps of able-bodied athletes. The "developing athletes" missed out on the big money deals, but most could procure clothing or wheelchair sponsors. I was in the room when Mark received his Nike shipment. Inspired by the excitement of free gear, he quickly tore open the boxes to find shirts, socks, some sweat pants and a new pair of Nike tennis shoes. He immediately pulled off his old pair, put on the new ones and we headed out for a full day of tennis.

That morning, Mark's spasms were more active than usual, but he accredited this to the excitement of playing a tough first round match. Enduring the aggravation of his legs jumping continuously, he played throughout the afternoon. Finally we withdrew to our room to prepare for the banquet that evening. Upon the removal of his shoes, Mark discovered that his toes were crumpled and contorted. Peeking inside, he realized he had forgotten to remove the tissue that comes in every pair.

Kids can provide some of the most heartfelt and humorous stories ever, and traveling with a junior wheelchair basketball team is a prime story machine. Taking the Rolling Rebels to the Pasadena Shoot-out, we had a very diverse group of kids that included traumatic injuries as well as birth defects. As every parent knows, the vibration of a vehicle has direct influence on kid's kidneys and bathroom breaks are a frequent part of travel. With a few of the kids needing to relieve themselves, we had pulled our odd-looking accessible bus into a service station. With only one bathroom, using the facility required a one-at-a-time procedure.

Bill, who had mild Cerebral Palsey, was first and since his disability was slight, if the distance was short, he could crawl on "all fours." He "crabbed" out of the bus, onto the gravel parking area and into the gas station. This was a shock to the attendant who looked back at us, wondering about our bus. Bill then crawled out of the store and back into the bus.

Willie then appeared and headed towards the store. Willie, who was thirty-five years old at the time, was born with dysfunction of the pituitary gland. This slowed his aging process, giving him the appearance of a 12-year-old. Born with curvature of the spine, which created a large deformity of his back, Willie also had visible atrophy of his hands and arms. With all due respect, to the every day person, he looked like he had escaped from the state fair. As he entered the station, used the restroom and returned, the attendant was even more confused.

The last person to use the restroom was Kerry, who was born with severe contractions of his lower limbs, which forced the doctors to conduct a double hip disarticulation (complete removal of his lower limbs). Basically Kerry was amputated from the *waist* down. From years of pushing a wheelchair and riding on a skateboard, he had a massive upper body and could actually run on his hands. Rather than inconvenience the group, Kerry got out of the bus, ran across the parking lot on his hands, leaned over on one hand to open the door, and entered to use the restroom. At this point, the grocery clerk was under major duress.

Once Kerry got back in the bus, we were able to enjoy the true meaning of "shock education" and a very attentive student. As we pulled away in laughter, we weren't too concerned with whether he pitied us because we were too involved in pitying him.

The Boston Marathon is an historic one hundred-year old race that attracts thousands of racers and supporters each year. The wheelchair division draws the biggest names and the fastest racers and does wonders for the promotion of wheelchair sports. Being more of a sprinter, I was very proud to have qualified, but was shocked when I witnessed a double amputee on a skateboard, warming up in the pre-race area of Hopkinton. How could they allow somebody on a skateboard in a race of this magnitude? Won't his participation hurt wheelchair racing? This isn't a freak show, aren't we supposed to be real athletes?

The starter eventually called us to the line and as the gun was fired, one hundred of the best wheelchair racers in the world hit the first hill, attaining speeds of up to forty miles an hour. In the early parts of the race, there were large packs of racers and lots of drafting, but as we spread out along roads of New England, the groups were reduced and I was separated from everyone. I was struggling at the infamous "heartbreak hill" in between Newton and Brookfine, which was at mile eighteen, and with my energy waning, I heard a sound that was very unfamiliar. Continuing to push, I looked over my shoulder and saw that guy on the skateboard coming up right behind me. In fact he was about to pass me. Since we were the only "athletes" around, I tucked in right behind him, attempting to take advantage of what little draft he provided. If any one of the racers had seen me do this, I would have been the laughing stock of the entire wheelchair sports world.

As we arrived in downtown Boston, the grade of the hill reversed, which favored my weight advantage and I quickly pulled away from "Skate Board Man" and the accompanying humility. Mocking this gentleman earlier, I was ironically reminded that no matter how insignificant someone might appear, every one of us has something to offer.

As previously mentioned, our Fresno Red Roller wheelchair basketball team was one of the best teams in the country. Winning a national championship in 1995, we boasted a diverse group of players and eventually changed the way wheelchair basketball was played. One of these players, Al, had a service dog named Zeus, which accompanied him wherever he went. We thought his need for a service dog was a bit of an act because Al was one of the top athletes in the world. What would he need a service dog for? We felt the dog could have been assigned to a more needy person, someone with more of a disability. He insisted that Zeus was necessary, but behind his back, he was the brunt of many jokes.

We were at a tournament in Las Vegas when between games, Al decided to take Zeus to a park next door. While Al was stretched out lying face down in the grass, Zeus was standing over him, licking the back of Al's neck. Unbeknownst to Al, the licking was only the "tip of the iceberg" as Zeus was actually involved in the canine's version of "the wild thing." And because of his paralysis, Al had no clue what was going on. For several minutes, Zeus was going to town, right there in the park, in front of all of Las Vegas, before Al caught on to his service dog's display of affection. We *rolled* in laughter and of course, during the "exhibition," had no intention of interrupting.

With all due respect, I enjoy giving my quadriplegic friends a hard time. As my dad says, "If I'm not teasing you, then something's wrong." Even after twenty-five years of living with a spinal cord injury, I am continuously amazed at what human beings with severe disabilities can do. Pilots, football coaches, families, the accomplishments are noteworthy. But for a person with limited hand function to go goose hunting demanded attention.

With a beautiful old bay house located near "geese-luring" rice fields, Doug had offered to take Mark and me goose hunting that fall. As a top racer, Mark had competed in many demanding events so we figured he knew his body well enough to adapt, but wielding a ten-gauge shotgun and absorbing its recoil was a different story. "Sort of" putting our worries at ease, that night Mark showed us the gloves he had developed using Velcro to attach the gun to his hands and the bent welding rod inside the finger sleeve to mimic the rigidity of a trigger finger. Without Velcro and "duck tape," people with spinal cord injuries might be extinct.

The next morning we loaded up and headed for the rice fields. Driving throughout different properties for hours, we finally found a huge group of birds in the middle of a large field. With Mark and me strategically positioned on the ground on one side of the field, Doug, and his partner Sammy, planned to drive to the other side and flush the birds in our direction. My responsibility was to help Mark get a good shot. But when he asked me to position behind him for back support while he fired his gun, a light went off in my head. I was about to prop against a guy who was completely paralyzed, who was attached with Velcro and welding rods to the largest shotgun made, in an attempt to shoot at thousands of geese that were about to fly right over our heads. I was "wheeling on thin ice."

After making peace with God, through trial and error, we discovered *what we thought* was the best way of stabilizing. Once set, we radioed our readiness, then heard the prompting blasts from the other side of the field. There is nothing quite like the sight of several thousand geese coming off the ground, and for a moment, my fear was forgotten. Reality set in though as the first of the "specs" and "snows" slumbered towards us thirty feet off the ground.

They were right on top of us when Mark fired his first shot. It sounded like a cannon and we were immediately pushed to one side. Listing, I thought it was over and that we were going to return to some form of sanity. Then Mark fired again. When Mark fired the third shot, we both collapsed sideways on the ground. At this point I was in full agreement with the Texas law that only allows three shells in a shotgun, because if there had been a fourth, somebody surely would have lost a foot. This was as close to a "fire fight" as I ever want to come. Raising up, I ascertained our casualties (there were none, including the geese), apologized for "forgetting" the extra shells and recommended we go in for lunch and a long, long nap.

Serving as the president of the Gulf Coast Chapter of Turning POINT, David, who was injured in a motorcycle accident, had been running geographic specific programs like the black drum fishing tournament for many years. David made his living running a shrimp and oyster operation, independently carrying out most of the job responsibilities himself. Participating in the tournament one year, I made note that the "flat boat" we were in, had dangerously low sides. For stability, we would position our selves in the rear of the boat, which allowed us to back our wheelchairs up against the 8" transom. As the guide pushed the boat to a faster speed, to compensate for the "tippiness," we would lean forward. Once he slowed, we would sit back up at our normal posture. We had stopped and started several times that morning and had become comfortable with the routine.

This particular time, the guide informed us that our next fishing spot was up ahead, so as we slowed, I relaxed and sat up to inspect the area. All of a sudden the guide changed his mind. Thrusting the engines to full capacity, the shift threw me backwards and I lost my balance. In a last ditch effort to save myself, I reached out but only grabbed a tackle box. Going twenty-five miles per hour across East Galveston Bay, I fell out of the boat.

My first reaction was to hold onto the engine, but brilliantly remembering that *boat motors had propellers*, I decided that wasn't a good idea. Luckily, we were going fast enough that I was swept away from the propeller. I plunged deep into the icy water, then quickly surfaced to see if anyone had noticed that I was gone. The boat was already on its way back as the guide was also in shock. He had no idea if I could swim. When we finally returned to the dock, the entire tournament had already heard the story.

Trust me, if you are ever in a "flat boat" fishing in the East Galveston Bay, or anywhere for that matter, paralyzed or not, watch yourself because you could get the surprise of your life. By the way, we never found my chair.

Hand cycles are the newest form of exercise equipment for the wheelchair user. With a multitude of styles, the hand bike pushes blood through our bodies with low impact aerobics; they are the future of longevity for the physically disabled. As with any motion machine, one must beware of the direction in which they are moving or grave consequences can occur.

Brent, a paraplegic who lived in Galveston, not only had a hand cycle, but lived in one of the best places in the world to cruise. Riding the sea wall overlooking Stewart Beach and its accompanying "scenery" definitely has its "perks." During a nice long ride,

Brent had become distracted by a couple of "perks" and was un-aware that his hand cycle had slightly drifted of course. Unfortu-nately, the sea wall at that location had no guardrail, which would have protected anyone from falling the twenty-five feet to the large granite boulders below. *Why would this story be in here?*

Going fifteen miles an hour, Brent went over the side and smashed headfirst onto the rocks. The accident hurt him badly, as he experienced several bangs, bruises and a compound fracture of his femur. Additionally, since no one saw him go over, until he could get the attention of a passer by, no one knew he was there. Finally someone heard his cries, looked over the edge and called 911. Brent was eventually flown in an emergency helicopter to the local hos-pital for some medical attention and a "defensive hand-cycling" re-fresher course.

The quadriplegic is a great example of adaptation and utilitar-ianism. They are absolutely the best in making the most out of lim-ited resources. This is especially evident in the sport of wheelchair tennis where muscles are refined into "maximum power output." No platitudes here, watching Quad Open champion Rick Draney play tennis goes beyond pure stroke execution. His game is a cele-bration of efficiency.

Due to the fact that quads have limited manual dexterity, hold-ing a tennis racket can be a problem. To solve this, athletic tape is wrapped with the sticky side up. This holds the hand to the racket and provides an adhesive surface, which aids in pushing the wheels.

We had sixty-five wheelchair tennis players attend our tennis camp at Coto de Casa, in Mission Viejo, California, and many who were quads. Since quadriplegia sometimes prohibits the body from perspiring, four of our athletes asked if they could skip the hot af-ternoon session and play late that night. The coaching staff agreed and informed the resort to turn on the lights on the back battery of courts. The concern of accessing the courts through several gates was dispelled when these players said they wouldn't "tape up" until they got there. That evening, we finished our late session, had some dinner and withdrew to rest for the demands of the next day.

Violating camp rules, the players who had asked about train-ing the previous night, arrived late to the morning session. When asked about their tardiness, they informed us that around midnight, the timer shut the lights off. Without sensation, they couldn't get their rackets off their hands. They couldn't find any edge to the tape.

And since they couldn't get their rackets off their hands, they had no way of opening the gates to leave the court. In other words, they were stuck there until two a.m. attached to their tennis rackets, chewing at the tape until one of them finally was able to remove his racket and help the others get free. *Have you ever seen a cat with a piece of tape stuck to its paw?*

Quickie Designs not only manufacturers and sells all kinds of wheelchairs, the company also demonstrates a belief in the remedial value of community-based recreational programs, and a conscience in the quality of life of people with disabilities. I have had the opportunity of conducting presentations and tennis camps around the world for Quickie, with many great stories, and Madison, Wisconsin, would be no different.

Upon our arrival, we were disappointed to find that the tennis courts had a gate designed to keep bicycles out of the facility. Functioning too efficiently, not only did the gate keep bicycles out, but it also made access for wheelchair users impossible. But we are a resilient group, so we transferred down to the ground and began breaking down our chairs. In assembly line fashion, we handed the individual parts to each other through the gate, then reassembled our rides on the other side. It took some time but we finally got all twenty players into the two-court facility and began the clinic.

Little did we know but a bog existed just behind the tennis facility, and as the sun went down, the biggest mosquitoes I have ever seen began infiltrating our clinic. I'm from Texas and I thought we had some big bugs, but that night I learned a lesson about mosquitoes from Wisconsin. At first what was a minor inconvenience eventually became too much to handle as we were overrun by the fiercest "blood suckers" I have ever seen. They were so bad we couldn't continue. We immediately made for the exit post haste, but as we arrived, we were reminded of the gate. We couldn't get off the courts. I am sure the discovering "scout mosquito," once he realized what he had found, said, "Just leave it, you aren't going to believe it. I'll explain it on the way."

It was one of the funniest and most panicked scenes I have ever witnessed. Here were twenty disabled individuals on the ground with broken down wheelchairs, slapping the air and cussing and trying to scoot through one little gate. We finally transferred into our cars, eliminated the remaining bugs that were brave enough to follow, and just waved at each other as we drove away.

Graphic Hygiene

> *Can you believe it? I had to add the word "gimp" to*
> *the Microsoft Word database of my computer.*
> *Someone call Bill Maher.*

No one really enjoys going graphic in this area, but I would be remiss if I a*void*ed venturing into the *bowels* of personal hygiene stories of the spinal cord injured. In matters of scheduling, when one is subject to the newly acquired random nature of the excretionary process, some pre-planning definitely bodes well. When it comes to a*void*ing an embarrassing situation involving pee or poop, or if there is uncertainty as to the accessibility of a facility, the adage "nothing in equals nothing out" has great value. Incidentally, if you are ever staying with a spinal cord injured person, don't drink out of any plastic cups or half-full bottles of Gatorade. One never really knows anything about their "prior life." Perhaps the following stories don't comfortably fit into what is accepted as societal norm, but they are revealing and hilarious. When we laugh we learn. I hope you can *hold it*.

In the context of *voiding*, let me open this section with a slang description of what we affectionately call plumbing. Plumbing refers to the various urinary collection devices used by some, to relieve incontinence. The "Big Three" plumbing pieces include some type of connection to the urethra, which involves either an indwelling catheter or a condom type collector, a collection device usually called a leg bag, and a piece of tubing that connects the two. Due to the varying types of systems, combined with the novice status of a newly injured person's *career*, there is great potential for a "situation" and a story.

Because of its newness in the 1980s, tennis saw several wheelchair players attempt to wear shorts as they had before their injury, but no one in their right mind was about to go out on a court with a "bag-o-pee" hanging from their leg. The challenge was to find a concealed plumbing system that would work with shorts. This created an era of "leg bag experimentation," which led to the wonderful discovery of the miniature bag. Not only did this device fit under shorts, but it also fit under a bathing suit as well. One must be aware though, as a submerged leg bag in a swimsuit brings on a subset of issues. Removal of any and all air from the unit, before venturing into the water, is mandatory. *Are you with me?*

Mark and I were sitting at the edge of the pool when we noticed a gorgeous girl wearing a robe coming out of her room. She descended down the steps and around the corner to the other end of the pool, where she sat and began splashing water on her self. With an interest, we both looked at each other, then Mark said, "Alright…I'll go." He took a deep breath, submerged himself and swam half way there. He came up for another breath, swam some more and arrived at our maiden. I then watched with a bit of envy, as he sat in the water and began carrying on a conversation, which quickly turned into laughter and obvious mutual enjoyment.

All of a sudden Mark just dove back into the water and began to swim back to me. As he swam up and settled, I said, "What happened?" He said everything was going fine until he noticed her looking down at his side. Disregarding her distraction, he continued to talk to her, but she just stared at the water next to him. Acquiescing, he finally looked and saw his leg bag bobbing next to him. It was half full of air and half full of pee. Rather than attempt to explain what it was, he just dove back into the water. As he finished telling me the story, I glanced back at the steps, and of course, she was gone.

I wore a leg bag at one time and had a similar yet unique situation. While training for a tennis tournament I was involved in some demanding lateral mobility. It required my entire focus. Working all out and sweating profusely, I was being pushed side to side by the head pro of the club. I remember him being a bit distracted during the lesson, spending more time looking at me rather than where I thought he should deliver the next ball. As I made another turn and headed back to the center of the court, I looked up and was shocked to find a leg bag with hosing attached to a condom catheter, lying right in the middle of the court.

Not knowing what to do… I just went by it. As I turned again, I slowed, then stopped, to see if it was mine. Denial is amazing.

Where else would a leg bag lying in the middle of the court come from? As a level of acceptance began to bring me back to reality, I noticed a trail of fluid re-tracing the exact circular path I had been traveling. It was definitely mine. Evidently the leg strap had come loose, which freed the half-full bag and allowed it to slip through my pants to the court. Once it started dragging, the tubing hadn't allowed it to fully pull out, which caused it to drag behind me, lengthening a little bit each time I pushed. I was basically hitting tennis balls for several minutes, pushing my chair and dragging a "bag-o-pee." No wonder the head pro was distracted. Saving me some embarrassment, he said, "Let's take a break, I'll get us some water." I quickly employed "gimp stealth," removed the unit from the court and told him I had to go home.

One time I pulled into a disabled parking place located right in front of a Walmart, but before I got my chair out, I began to cath myself. Just as I inserted the catheter, a good samaritan police officer, who was protecting the spaces for qualified handicapped individuals, came up to inquire whether I really needed the parking spot. Arriving at my window and catching me in mid-cath, he quickly inferred that I was legitimate.

Carol had just completed the Oita Marathon in Japan and was on her way back to the States. While she was waiting to board the plane, some of the passengers and crew recognized her from the Japanese television and newspaper coverage. This resulted in a little more notoriety as she became the plane's superstar.

During the flight Carol decided to celebrate her success by having a glass of wine, but early in the flight, had to use the restroom. Aerodynamically designed, jets do not entertain the luxury of space, which makes accessibility difficult. Acknowledging her extreme urge to use the restroom, Carol transferred down to the aisle and started scooting towards the toilet. Unfortunately she was too late, as her bladder spasmed, and not only did she pee all over her self, but she left a large puddle right in the middle of the aisle. Attempting to avoid being associated with the puddle, she increased her scooting pace. Just as she had moved a few feet, a voice came over the loud speaker and said, "Ladies and gentlemen, we would like to bring your attention to a star we have on board that won the marathon in the wheelchair division. Please give Carol a round of applause for her super accomplishment." Carol said heads on both sides of the aisle peeked around their seats to see her sitting in a big "puddle-o-pee" on the floor. She just smiled and waved.

Wheelchair gimps don't have the luxury of using the bathroom in the outdoors as able-bodied people. Certainly peeing in the woods is difficult, but when it comes to good old number two, there can be some real headaches. If we do venture into an outdoor situation and have to take care of "The Big Easy," sometimes it leaves us with disgusting alternatives and "cross-over" consequences. This was the case when Greg went fishing at Bason's Landing in Southern Louisiana.

After eating etouffe, jambalaya, and fried oysters, Greg incurred an unwelcome case of the *paraplegia demon*, which resulted in a "situation." Planning to fish for the entire day made taking care of the "situation" a priority. Greg's options were to drop his bum in the frigid water and rinse out or venture into the nasty old outhouse. At least the outhouse was dry, had a seat and was private, so he selected the latter. After dealing with the "situation," Greg attempted to turn on the water to clean himself but discovered that the faucet was non-functional. With no other viable option, Greg rinsed his pants in the toilet, then cleaned his hands the best he could. This was done without the luxury of soap or a hand towel. As soon as he came out of the outhouse, Greg's dad said, "Come here son, I want you to meet Mr. Rancier. He's the director of the bank in Baton Rouge." As Mr. Rancier held out his hand, *what else could Greg do?*

Speaking of directors, once I was standing on my long leg braces outside a major hospital, in discussion with the director of marketing about the possibility of expanding their recreational programs. When standing on braces, it behooves a paralyzed person to "self-check" frequently as a "situation" can happen without notice. During our conversation, I casually glanced down and to my surprise, I noticed three little familiar looking "pooh balls" right next to my feet. Realizing their "origin of species," I had no other choice but to lift my foot, and stand on them. Now I couldn't move and I was going to stand there as long as it took for her to leave. Feeling like she was speaking to me from *a hundred yards away*, I lost the ability to focus on anything she said. The only thing on my mind was to end our dialogue so she would leave. After what seemed like *weeks*, she finally ran out of topics and bid me farewell, leaving me to swallow my pride, sit down and look for a stick.

To some, it's a form of competition, but in my opinion, auto racing isn't a sport. Embracing the idea of an oil change every 3000 miles, I only care that cars work, not how they work. While enjoying the south of France after a tournament, in a weak moment I attended a Grand Prix auto-racing event. I wasn't going to listen to French announcers describe cars going around the track all day, so to break the monotony, I headed towards the concession stand. Adding to the ripe grapes from the day before, my food consumption stimulated an urgent need to visit the "loo," where I learned that eastern toilets were invented in, but not limited to, the east. An eastern toilet is nothing more than a porcelain hole in the ground with "ready-set-go" places on either side for your feet.

Acknowledging the fact that a paraplegic must sit, regardless, eastern style toilets are considered *very* disabled unfriendly. In order to carry out the necessary requirements of "The Grand Pooh Bah," I had to transfer to the floor of an open stall, balance myself over the hole with one hand, and attend to the literal task-at-hand with the other. If this wasn't degrading enough, in the middle of the *paraplegia demon*, I noticed there wasn't any toilet paper. I had to use my free hand to retrieve my Swiss Army Knife, cut my underwear up into little sections and wipe up.

I finally finished with a public display worthy of mention in a future issue of *Gimp Adaptation Magazine*. As I was exiting, the staff person had the audacity to ask me for a contribution. The only contribution I had for him was already there.

In leaving the 500 fans watching the final of the Japan Open, I did have a little guilt, but my need to use the restroom minimized my remorse. With the promise of edibility, the sushi and other various items I had eaten during our trip had brought on *the demon*, so I asked for permission, then left the court to relieve myself. Sweating profusely, I was simultaneously wiping my forehead and my bottom. When I transferred off the toilet, I could still distinguish a faint smell of *the demon*, so I began a "self-check." I checked my hands, my pants, even my chair, but I couldn't seem to find it anywhere. The tennis official waiting outside kept saying, "Mr. Landy, are you OK, it's time to come now, Mr. Landyson?"

Knowing that somewhere on me was a "little brown badge-of-courage" that probably wouldn't be understood if discovered by a fan, regretfully I was about to give up and return to the court. As I washed my hands, I glanced into the mirror and to my surprise, there it was, a betraying speck, just under my nose that carried an aroma of a much larger scale. I quickly wiped it off and thanked God for sparing me the lesson in humility.

Another time I was fishing with my good buddy David at Caddo Lake in East Texas. David had his special "watermelon" colored worm that was nailing the black bass. He would catch a fish, brag about how much better of a fisherman he was, replace the prized bait back on his hook, and recast out into the lily pads. I was certainly pleased when he dropped the worm into the water, out of his reach. Now it was my turn.

With plans of holding it hostage and ending his attack on my manhood, I guided the boat over to the worshiped bait. At first I tried to retrieve it using a fishing pole but it was just beyond my reach. Drifting closer, I realized that if I really stretched, I could grab it with my hand. I transferred down to the bottom of the boat and with some *straining*, I leaned way over the side and nabbed the bait. After toying with David for moment, I eventually tossed it back to him and we throttled onward to another location.

A good boat captain continuously checks his craft so while we were cruising, I began to inspect our vessel. That's when I saw it, right there on the floor of the boat, a big ol' paraplegic terd ball, lying there like a mini loaf of bread. Out loud, I said "Whoa." David turned around and said, "What is it?" I thought for a moment, then said, "Nothing." When he turned back around, I picked up the "Ruthie" and cleared it.

Most of the time the paralyzed person isn't even aware that a fart is about to occur. I was getting some work done on my shoulder in Sydney in the U.S.O.C. Medical tent. As I transferred up onto the table, I had no idea it was going to happen but out of the blue, I ripped a ripper. I tried to explain that due to my paralysis I wasn't aware, therefore I couldn't control it, but my argument was denied, so I apologized and just laughed. Here are a few more of the "stools and dribulations" we occasionally go through when things don't go as planned. The following *offerings* are about the *gas we pass.*

240

Pressurization of the cabin fluctuates during the flight, which expands and contracts the abdomens of every person on the plane. Once on the ground, the created spaces are collapsed, which give birth to a potpourri of methane-based contributions. It happens to all of us. I have often wondered what people think as they deplane and experience this confined "tapestry of air." Here is this trail of people leaving among varying whiffs, with a disabled person sitting in their seat, waiting for the carry-off crew to arrive. I'm sure the gimp gets the blame. People walking by thinking, "Whew, handicapped people, there ought to be a law."

I will never forget my first date after I returned home from rehab. At that time my transfers from positions near the height of my chair were satisfactory, but when it came to anything down low, it was a strain. Knowing I must first do the chivalrous thing, I went to my date's house to meet her parents. We sat on the couch and made small talk while we snacked lightly. It's the eating that gets me. Once I eat, the system is stimulated and I am guaranteed one of the three "p's." I either have to pee, poot, or poop. Finishing our conversation and getting ready to leave, I pulled my chair over and prepared to transfer. Just like my therapist told me, I did a little silent 1-2-3, ducked my head and *pushed forward*. All of a sudden, there she blows-foghorn-ship horn-air-horn, like I "horned" the place, I farted right in her parents' faces. I tried to explain but I know they didn't believe me. The people who encounter this and don't believe us must think we are pigs. And of course the *dancing* begins.

After working with Tim, a sales representative of a company we both worked for, I was standing on my braces and relaxing in the middle of his kitchen. It was very nice of Tim to invite me into his home that was located up in the mountains over looking Denver. With a light snow coming down, Tim had put on a fire and he and his wife were preparing dinner. I was talking with them and stretching my legs, when I became aware of a "space" in my descending colon. I should have known better than to stretch my quadriceps by doing a pelvic thrust, and especially after eating Buffalo steaks the night before, but when I did...I did. Fortunately it was a "silencer" so as long as it could pass the smell test, I would be in the clear.

But like a swarm of locust coming out of a field of corn, the awful odor lifted through my pants and overtook me. This created a major "gimp survival moment." At first I wondered, "Do I risk not telling them and hope the smell goes unnoticed?" This wasn't really an option because it was extremely potent and had a high chance of detection. Risking being considered a pig, "Do I tell them and hope of compassion and an understanding of my lack of control?" This seemed like a worse option. As I was about to confess, I glanced towards their two-year old son Andrew, who was playing on the floor of the kitchen. When I turned back to see if it had reached Tim yet, I received some more good news as I noticed Sam, their eight-year old yellow Labrador, lying at the other end of the room. I was OK. I had lots of cover.

Suddenly, Tim dropped his eyebrows and his demeanor took on a concerned countenance. No longer was he interested in chopping green peppers; he quickly developed a need to "evaluate the environment." As I waited in "gimp stealth," Tim looked at Andrew, then at Sam and said, "Sam, get outside!" After our meal, I went outside to where Sam was lying in his doghouse in the snow and sincerely apologized. He wouldn't even look at me.

I will spare the remaining notes here as the point has been made. If we cannot laugh at ourselves, the path we grow will be slow.

> *You grow up on the day you have your first*
> *real laugh at yourself.*
> ✳ *Ethel Barrymore*

Chapter Twenty-One

Along the Way

I'm impressed. To have read this far, you have obviously learned something about persistence and patience. The three sections of this book represent three very important principles.

When we face challenges, *pushing forward* begins by finding *value* in ourselves. No matter what happens, if we focus on a positive attitude, become accountable and do our best, win or lose, we will survive. It will work out. The "simple secret" is to believe we are worth it and to do something about it.

> *The used key is always bright.*
> ✳ *Benjamin Frankin*

Secondly, we are surrounded by extraordinary stories with moving messages; it's in the *listening* that messages become powerful. Notice them, hold on to them and let their strength *push you forward*.

> *Lynette, a spinal cord victim from a car accident said,*
> *"It was all about my shoes. I had 200 pair of shoes and*
> *was frequently late for work because I was so worried*
> *about which pair to wear, it was my biggest dilemma.*
> *Now if I could just get my shoes on by myself*
> *I would be happy."*

And finally, about disabilities, whatever that word means. Using a wheelchair is like being bald, having freckles or being impatient; it's just a feature, a characteristic of the person. Personally I would rather be in a wheelchair than be allergic to shellfish, but we all have our challenges. It's our acceptance of others, our ability to be compassionate, with all the inhabitants of our planet that will make living life agreeable.

> *I learned that my disability was not a defining*
> *principle of who I am, rather just a*
> *characteristic of my being.*
> ✳ *Eight-time Boston Marathon winner Jean Driscoll*

As I write today, Lance Armstrong won his second Tour de France. He was a great cyclist before he contracted cancer but the adversity of a life-threatening disease brought out the best in this challenge-based fighter. Being "ready to die" didn't make him weaker; it polished what counted.

When we are challenged by change, there is a tendency to listen to the voice of doubt, which always makes us disabled. We do not acquiesce to that voice. We join the fight. We look way down inside beyond the fringes for something to clutch too. And it's there that we find a fighter, a victor…a gladiator who is really a part of us, waiting for the summons. At times it takes this uncomfortable fringe, that "wounded bear" place as Brad Gilbert, Andre Agassi's coach calls it, to awaken the competitor. But it's the participation in the fight that brings forth value and self-fulfillment. Good friend and mother of three, Lorilyn Braymer said, "At some point we just have to get on with it." I love the reality of her gentle yet firm position.

> *It will either be done or it won't, there is no try.*
> ✳ *Yoda*

If I was asked today if I would want to walk, well, of course, I would. That bale of hay didn't hit me that hard. Walking is intrinsic, common and a part of life. Like money though, being able to walk is not necessary to live a quality life. Walking is less important than health, family or a spiritual relationship. The quality of my laughter and of my tears has been a contributing factor to my emotional and spiritual growth, which would have been less than if I had not had to *scrap.*

Life is about adjusting, adapting to change, about finding a way to make it work. It's about evolving. The dinosaurs aren't extinct; you can find them everywhere, the ones that changed. Having the good fortune to be able to switch lenses, to adjust and know gratitude, is the most important thing in the world.

> *The paradox of life is, sometimes it takes a lifetime to figure it out.*
> ✳ *Tina Dale*

Life will provide many opportunities and disappointments. There will be wins and losses, successes and failures, but one thing is certain. It will move on. When life doesn't agree and *seems* to push in from all directions, what choice do we have? Make the decision, cowboy up and *push forward!*

I hope to see you somewhere along the way!

—Randy Snow